ON EQUAL TERMS

A Thesaurus for Nonsexist Indexing and Cataloging

Compiled by Joan K. Marshall

Neal·Schuman Publishers, Inc.

Published by Neal-Schuman Publishers, Inc.
P.O. Box 1687, FDR Station, New York, N.Y. 10022
Copyright © 1977 by Joan K. Marshall
Printed and bound in the United States of America

Library of Congress Cataloging in Publication

Marshall, Joan K.
   On equal terms.

   1. Subject headings.   I. Title
Z695.M36   025.3'3   77-8987
ISBN 0-918212-02-2
ISBN 0-918212-03-0 pbk.

Contents

Foreword

    To be effectively identified and utilized, the large and fast-growing corpus of women's materials requires full and unbiased access through library catalogs and periodical indexes. However, existing subject-schema—being variously archaic, male-slanted, imprecise, and incomplete—do not permit such access. Instead, they commonly inhibit it. This thesaurus should thus prove extremely useful to catalogers, indexers, and—ultimately—the public. It represents not merely "another" subject-heading list, nor a sterile, irrelevant "exercise," but rather a practical, truly authoritative, long-needed tool for making women-related books, pamphlets, magazines, films, tapes, kits, and records genuinely and immediately accessible to the people who want them. Further, it's an excellent model for unbiased indexing, providing comprehensive, multilevel cross-references and demonstrating that subject descriptors *can* be at once fair, accurate, and helpful.

    A Council on Library Resources grant enabled Joan Marshall to undertake this project. And she was precisely the right person—indeed, the *best* person—to do it. An experienced, highly respected cataloger, she has written extensively and creatively on many aspects of subject analysis, founded the SRRT Task Force on Women's Committee on Sexist Subject Headings, which she continues to head, and has served with distinction on the Catalog Code Revision Committee. I know her to be an outstanding professional, dedicated feminist, brilliant critic, and sensitive human being. I heartily endorsed her CLR project when it was first proposed in late 1974, and I'm delighted now to commend its outcome as a major contribution to subject cataloging theory and practice alike.

Sanford Berman
Head Cataloger
Hennepin County Library
Edina, Minnesota

Editor, *HCL cataloging bulletin*

Acknowledgements

Members of the Committee on Sexism in Subject Headings

Elizabeth Dickinson, Broward County Library System
Margaret Myers, American Library Association
Joan K. Marshall, Chairperson, Brooklyn College Library

The thesaurus was compiled with the critical assistance of the following librarians and feminists and with the less formal assistance of many friends and colleagues:

Ann Bein
University of California,
Los Angeles

Sanford Berman
Hennepin County Public Library

Sherrill Cheda
Seneca College of Applied Arts and Technology

Doris Clack
School of Library Science,
Florida State University

Elizabeth Dickinson
Broward County Library System

Elizabeth Futas
Queens College

Elizabeth Herman
University of California,
Los Angeles

Holly Harkness
Minnesota Women's Center

Linda Lewis
University of New Mexico

Linda Lubitz
Baltimore Hebrew College

Mary McKenney
San Francisco, Calif.

Beth McNeer
Ohio State University

Linda Parker
University of Kansas

Felice R. Reisler
University of Wisconsin

Linda Running
Hennepin County Public Library

Anita Schiller
University of California,
San Diego

Judith Shoffit
Texas Woman's University

Anne Thorsen Truax
University of Minnesota

Buckwheat Turner
Montgomery, N.Y.

Ruth Ulman
H.W. Wilson Co.

Helen Wheeler
Baton Rouge, La.

Laura X
Women's History Research Center

Arlene Zuckerman
University of California,
Los Angeles

Work on the thesaurus was partially supported by a grant from the Council on Library Resources.

Preface

The consciousness-raising of women toward sex bias in language and its effect upon their position in society began in the late 1960's. The consciousness-raising of the American library community toward bias in the *Library of Congress Subject Heading List* (hereafter referred to as *LCSH*) began at about the same time. Some of us, who are both women and librarians, had our consciousness doubly raised, and in spring 1974 we organized a Committee on Sexism in Subject Headings under the sponsorship of the American Library Association's SRRT Task Force on Women.

The first task the Committee set itself was the development of a report documenting sexism in the *LCSH* since that list is the most widely used source, both nationally and internationally, of subject descriptors. We were not the first critics of the list. It had long been criticized for exhibiting bias—either actively through the use of biased terminology, or passively through the absence of terms to adequately cover concepts. The Library of Congress (hereafter referred to as LC) has not been impervious to this criticism, but its response is usually slow and often inadequate.

During the Annual Conference of the American Library Association in July 1974, we presented our report on sex bias in the *LCSH* to the Association's RTSD Subject Analysis Committee and, through that Committee, to the Library of Congress. In the statement prepared by Elizabeth Dickinson as part of the report, five categories of problems were identified: the Man/Woman generic problem, subsuming terminology, the modifier tactic, separate and unequal treatment, and omissions.

As a result of our presentation and previous criticism, LC changed its primary heading WOMAN to WOMEN. This change resolved, at least, the problem of the generic form being used as the general term and thereby eliminated such anomalies as WOMAN—RIGHTS OF WOMEN from the list. They also changed all *as* forms under women; (i.e. *LCSH* occupational headings for women were constructed WOMEN AS LIBRARIANS [ACCOUNTANTS, LAWYERS, ETC.]), and other decided improvements were made.

But the changes were not very far-ranging. FEMINISM was established as a heading, but WOMEN'S LIBERATION MOVEMENT was canceled (supposedly because LC catalogers would never know which one to assign). The subdivision SOCIAL AND MORAL QUESTIONS was retained for pre-1940's feminist works. (In actual fact, an examination of LC's catalog reveals that the heading is still assigned to many post-1940's feminist works.) DELINQUENT WOMEN was changed to FEMALE OFFENDERS (which I do not like, although it is a decided improvement), but REFORMATORIES FOR WOMEN, rather than prisons, was retained.

Ed Blume, Chief of LC's Subject Cataloging Division, said at that 1974 meeting that LC could not undertake the far-ranging review of its subject headings which the Committee believed to be essential for real change to be made. He would, however, consider making additional changes suggested by us if we would establish these in priority order. The Committee considered and rejected this possibility for two reasons.

First, we recognized that LC was tied to its catalog. Suggestions for changes in and additions to the *LCSH* would necessarily be evaluated in terms of the effect such changes and additions would have on LC's catalog rather than only for their validity. For instance, the LC decision to retain WOMEN—SOCIAL AND MORAL QUESTIONS for pre-1940's works was undoubtedly based on internal considerations. LC assigned this heading to both feminist writings and to Victorian maunderings on the effect upon the sacred institutions of womanhood and motherhood—as Victorian men saw those institutions—of women assuming a genuine place in society. If the heading had not been retained, LC would have had to recatalog and sort out the anti-feminist tracts from the feminist tracts.

Second, we recognized that the problem of bias in the *LCSH* is much broader than sex bias, and that what was needed was a reevaluation of the principles used in establishing *LCSH* subject headings rather than a band-aid solution to its sex bias. The Committee, therefore, set as its second task the development of principles for the establishment of nonbiased subject headings relating to people and peoples. The principles were presented for endorsement to the American Library Association's RTSD Subject Analysis Committee and, through that Committee, to the Library of Congress during the Association's Annual Conference in July 1975. They have been recommended for use in libraries by the Subject Analysis Committee, and they have been accepted for use, where appropriate, by LC.

The next stage in our effort to improve access to materials by, about, and of concern to women was an extensive examination of LC's collection and cataloging of relevant materials. Supported by a grant from the Council on Library Resources, I spent September through November 1975 examining the files at the Library of Congress under headings beginning with the words WOMAN and WOMEN and selected related headings (e.g. DELINQUENT GIRLS, MARRIAGE, SEX DISCRIMINATION, SEX ROLE, etc.). I compared the descriptive cataloging (i.e. the transcription of the title page and cataloger's notes about the work) with the subject headings assigned by LC. If I believed, on the basis of that information, that a work was undercataloged or miscataloged, I copied the LC card and, on a selective basis, examined the work itself. I copied approximately 1500 cards. These were merely representative; once an area of undercataloging was determined and the need for a subject heading established, I did not copy all of the cards which demonstrated the need. I examined approximately 500 titles. (I might have examined more, but LC had a "not on shelves" problem of some dimensions at that time.)

The purpose of the examination of LC's collection and subject heading assignment policy was the development of a thesaurus of indexing terms for materials, by, about, or of concern to women. The thesaurus that developed is somewhat broader than that; since we were suggesting so many changes in *LCSH* headings relating to women, we took the opportunity to suggest other changes which we believe are necessary to unbias the catalog and to improve access.

We were committed to enlisting as much participation as possible in the compilation of the thesaurus. We believed, and believe, that only with wide participation would we be adhering to the principles we developed and, further, that only with wide participation would our work have impact on the Library of Congress. The first draft of the thesaurus was distributed in January 1976, prior to the American Library Association Midwinter Meeting, to 14 librarians for criticism, additions, changes, or other suggestions; eight of the 14 responded. The second draft was distributed in June 1976, prior to the American Library Association Annual Conference, to 41 persons, librarians and others, concerned with access to women's materials; 20 of the 41 responded. The Committee also held open meetings at the American Library Association Annual and Midwinter meetings in 1975 and 1976.

The thesaurus that follows is based upon the principles developed by the Committee, upon the examination of relevant areas in LC's extensive collection, and upon the collective judgment of concerned librarians and feminists.

Joan K. Marshall
May 1977

Part One

Introduction

Sexism and Language

Human beings do not live in the objective world alone, nor alone in the world of social activity as ordinarily understood, but are very much at the mercy of the particular language which has become the medium of expression for their society. It is quite an illusion to imagine that one adjusts to reality essentially without the use of language and that language is merely an incidental means of solving specific problems of communication or reflection. The fact of the matter is that the "real world" is to a large extent unconsciously built up on the language habits of the group. . . . We see and hear and otherwise experience very largely as we do because the language habits of our community predispose certain choices of interpretation. *Edward Sapir, 1929.*[1]

Women's interest in the relationship of sex and language has been growing steadily since the late 1960's. *She said/he said*[2], a bibliography of sex differences in language, lists 147 items; 81 of these date from 1970, 34 date from the years between 1961 and 1970. Current investigations by linguists and sociologists support the belief, often expressed by feminists, that language is a significant factor in shaping our perception of the world.

We are all taught in early childhood that father and similar humans are men and that mother and similar humans are women. The concept of *man* as a generic term for all humans is not introduced until some later period, at which time, unlike most learning experiences which build upon what is already known, we are expected to be able to absorb an apparent contradiction: man is also woman. Studies reveal that the definition learned initially, man equals males, is never fully replaced by the dictionary definition.

In 1973, Alleen Pace Nilsen conducted a study with 100 nursery age through seventh grade school children. She found that *man,* used generically, was interpreted by a majority of the children, of both sexes, as meaning male.[3] A more extensive study was conducted by Linda Harrison in 1974. Approximately 500 junior high school boys and girls were asked to illustrate seven statements on early human activity—the use of tools, plant cultivation, pottery making, etc. One group of students received statements worded in terms of the generic and *he;* a second group received statements worded in terms of *people, humans,* and *they;* a third group received statements worded in terms of *men and women* and *they.* In each of the groups, a majority of the students of both sexes drew pictures of males only oftener than of females only, although the last group did include the greatest number of illustrations of females. In the first group, 49 percent of the boys and 11 percent of the girls drew male figures only—even to illustrate the statement on early infant care![4]

Harrison's study demonstrates that the language of textbooks and of the school room—early *man,* Cro-Magnon *man, man* invents the wheel— so inculcates a male image that that image takes precedence even when students are given neutral statements such as *humans* or *people* or statements reminding them that there are both men and women in the world. And our inability to absorb the definition of *man* as a generic for humankind is not resolved by greater maturity or advanced education.

In a study conducted at Drake University in 1972 approximately 300 college students were asked to select illustrations for a sociology textbook that was being prepared for publication. Half of the students were given chapter headings that used the generic in the title: *social man, political man, economic man, industrial man.* The other half were given corresponding headings that did not use the generic: *social behavior, political behavior, economic behavior, industrial life.* Students of both sexes selected significantly fewer pictures depicting the activities of women for the chapters that used the generic in the title.[5]

These studies clearly indicate that the dictionary definition of man as a generic for humankind is merely a definition. The idea that *man* equals *man and woman* has not been absorbed by human consciousness. In *Words and women,* Miller and Swift remark: "One may be saddened but not surprised at the statement 'man is the only primate that commits rape.' Although, as commonly understood, it can apply to only half the human population, it is nevertheless semantically acceptable. But 'man, being a mammal, breast-feeds his young' is taken as a joke.'"[6] It is a joke and totally unacceptable semantically since *man* does not mean *man and woman* except in the dictionary!

The use of *man* is misleading and inaccurate; conceptually, the image conveyed is that of a male human being. Since the use of the generic conceptually excludes women, women's role in the development of humankind, in history, in the arts, in society is either ignored or belittled. The adjustment to the generic is an important element in the sex role socialization of children. Only with effort are girls able to insinuate themselves into the images presented in the school room and by society at large:

> Even if the female child understands that yes, she too is part of man, she must still leap the hurdles of all those other terms that she knows from her experience refer to males only. When she is told that we are all brothers, that the brotherhood of man includes sisters, and that the faith of our fathers is also the faith of our mothers, does she really believe it? How does she internalize these concepts? . . . By an act of will? By writing it on the blackboard a hundred and fifty times?[7]

The linguistic exclusion of the female is not only limited to sex-linked words such as *man* and *brotherhood;* it is popularly extended to neutral words such as *people* and *Americans* and is semantically acceptable although incorrect. Miller and Swift cite a television commentator: "People won't give up power. They'll give up anything else first—money, home, wife, children—but not power," and a sociologist: "Americans of higher status have more years of education, more children attending college, less divorce, lower mortality, better dental care, and less chance of having a fat wife."[8]

Women, and some men, have come to recognize that the "real world" referred to by Sapir, the world which has been "built up on the language habits of the group," is a sexist world. English language habits limit women's full participation in society. The limits are often imposed subtly; prescriptive grammarians have required the use of male sex-linked words to describe all of humankind. These words conceptually exclude women and impede the development in women of a positive self-image and thereby limit her conception of her role in society. If man is the norm, woman becomes the other.

Limits are also imposed overtly. The use of sex-linked words such as mailmen and congressmen, in the mistaken notice that this is an extension of the male generic rule, to describe occupations or activities which are engaged in by both women and men is an overt limitation on women's role. The use of the sex-linked word denies the fact of, and calls into question the apropriateness of, women's involvement in such activities. If women engage in activities not described by sex-linked words, such as writing poetry or working for suffrage, society feels compelled to identify this deviance from the norm by coining words with *-ess* or *-ette* endings.

But whether the limits are imposed subtly or overtly, the language supports the cultural norm: man is active, woman is passive. This particular norm is now being challenged by both women and men. The question becomes: must the language change if the norm is to change? Benjamin Whorf, a linguist, writing in 1940 would answer, yes:

> Which was first: the language patterns or the cultural norms? In main they have grown up together, constantly influencing each other. But in this partnership the nature of the language is the factor that limits free plasticity and rigidifies channels of development in the more autocratic way. This is so because a language is a system, not just an assemblage of norms. Large systematic outlines can change to something really new only very slowly, while many other cultural innovations are made with comparative quickness. Language thus represents the mass mind; it is affected by inventions and innovations but affected little and slowly, whereas to inventors and innovators it legislates with the decree immediate.[9]

As Whorf points out, changing language is not an easy task. But if we believe that language supports cultural norms which we reject, we must work consciously toward bringing that change about. *On Equal Terms* is a conscious effort to provide an alternative to—and to change the vocabulary of—the most widely used source of subject descriptors, the *Library of Congress Subject Heading List,* with the expectation that such change will affect the mass mind—even if only a "little and slowly."

References:

1. Sapir, Edward. "The status of linguistics as a science," *Language,* 5, 1929; reprinted in his *Selected writings,* David G. Mandelbaum, ed. 1963. p. 162.

2. Henley, Nancy & Barrie Thorne, comps. *She said/he said; an annotated bibliography of sex differences in language, speech, and nonverbal communication.*

KNOW, Inc., 1975. (First published as the bibliography in *Language and sex: difference and dominance*. 1975).

3. Miller, Casey & Kate Swift. *Words and women; new language in new times*. Anchor Press/Doubleday, 1975. p. 24.

4. Harrison, Linda. "Cro-Magnon woman—in eclipse," *The Science teacher*, April 1975, p. 8–11.

5. Schneider, Joseph W. & Sally L. Hacker. "Sex role imagery and the use of the generic 'man' in introductory texts," *American sociologist*, 8, No. 8, 1973, p. 12–18.

6. Miller & Swift, *op. cit.*, p. 25–26.

7. *Ibid.*, p. 36–37.

8. *Ibid.*, p. 37.

9. Whorf, Benjamin Lee. "Science and linguistics," *Technology review*, 42, No. 6, April 1940; reprinted in his *Language, thought, and reality*, John B. Carroll, ed. 1956. p. 156.

Principles for Establishing Subject Headings Relating to People and Peoples

Background

The underlying philosophy—perhaps too grand a word—of *LCSH* subject heading-establishment was set forth by David Haykin in his *Subject headings; a practical guide*. I am not laying blame for the *LCSH* bias at Haykin's feet; in 1951, when his work was published, the *LCSH* with all of its faults had been in existence for a long time. His guidelines merely presented a rationale for an existing document; unfortunately, the rationale, once stated, was not challenged as untenable until recently.

Haykin acknowledges that we lack knowledge of the probable approach of various classes and categories of readers to the subject catalog. But, he states, although we lack this knowledge, the reader is the focus in all cataloging principles and practice, and "all other considerations, such as convenience and the desire to arrange entries in some logical order, are secondary to the basic rule that the heading . . . should be that which the reader will seek in the catalog, if we know or can presume what the reader will look under."[1] Our presumption, apparently, is to be based upon our acknowledged lack of knowledge of what to presume.

Haykin continues: "To the extent that headings represent the predilection of the cataloger in regard to terminology and are dictated by conformity to a chosen logical pattern, as against the likely approach of the reader resting on psychological rather than logical grounds, the subject catalog will lose in effectiveness and ease of approach."[2]

The guideline dictates that we abandon logic and consistency in favor of an unknown reader's psychological approach to the catalog. The basis for subject heading establishment, therefore, is wholly subjective, and it is a subjectivity once removed: a subject heading is established on the basis of what a subject cataloger thinks a reader will think. This is a rather fuzzy basis for establishing subject headings, but fuzziness is not the worst of the guideline's faults.

The application of the guideline requires the construction of a hypothetical reader. Such hypothesizing may be necessary in selecting, for instance, a heading from among synonyms; the construction of the hypothesis must be limited to considerations such as whether the subject heading list is designed to serve the general public or the scientific community, the adult or the juvenile user. Examination of the *LCSH*, however, reveals that considerations of nationality, ethnic background, religion, and sex have been factors which have entered into the construction, over the years, of LC's hypothetical reader.

The reader has been identified as American/ Western European, Christian, white, heterosexual, and male. The identification is not surprising since it reflects the point of view that has been dominant for so long in our society. But that point of view does not accurately reflect the world we live in. Non-Americans/Western Europeans, non-Christians, non-whites, non-heterosexuals, and non-males exist in numbers and have always existed in numbers. In addition, they are becoming more and more of a force in society. Ideally, the "nons" should not have had to become a force before bias was identified and corrected in the *LCSH*. But then, ideally, there should be no such concept as "nons."

Ideals aside, one fact remains. The attempt to identify a single reader, and therefore the creation of a hypothetical norm, has resulted in subject descriptors which serve some and disserve or underserve the many. Subject descriptors must reflect the multiplicity of points of view that our users hold. The objection to subject headings reflecting a multiplicity of viewpoints—the reader's expectations concerning access will not be met—is not valid. Which reader's expectations? We have many readers, and each of their expectations concerning access is likely to be different. I sincerely doubt that the heading WOMAN—SOCIAL AND MORAL QUESTIONS met any user's expectations!

Libraries are social institutions in a multicultural society and as such have a responsibility to serve all elements in society. We must keep all of our readers in focus. Libraries are also educational institutions. We do not disserve our users if, in not meeting their expectations concerning access, we instruct them (and ourselves) in nonbiased terminology.

With these considerations in mind—the rejection of the hypothetical reader and of the idea that we would meet expectations concerning access if those expectations perpetuated bias—the Committee developed the following principles for the establishment of subject headings relating to people and peoples.

The Principles

1. The authentic name of ethnic, national, religious, social, or sexual groups should be established if such a name is determinable. If a group does not have an authentic name, the name preferred by the group should be established. The determination of the authentic or preferred name should be based upon the literature of the people themselves (not upon outside sources or experts), upon organizational self-identification, and/or upon group member experts.

For example, the names of indigenous American and African peoples established by the Library of Congress are very often derogatory corruptions of these people's real names. (*Kaffir*, which was changed recently, is the equivalent of *nigger* in the United States.) The corruptions were established by the ancestors of LC's hypothetical readers; they are terms with which most of us have become familiar and under which most of us would probably expect to find access to material. But these names are not authentic. People have a right to be called by their own name, and, most significantly, the names established by the Library of Congress very often perpetuate preconceptions that reinforce prejudice.

2. In establishing subdivisions for use with the names of people or peoples, consider the connotation, in addition to the denotation, of the wording and structure of the subdivision. Avoid words which connote inferiority or peculiarity. In establishing subdivisions for concepts applicable to all classes of people, avoid variations in the structure of the subdivision under certain people or peoples. Avoid American/Western European ethnocentrism. Avoid value-loaded words; aim for neutrality.

Many subdivisions now applied to minority peoples and to women (a majority with minority status) support the assumptions of the majority (LC's hypothetical reader). Clear examples of such support were the abandoned forms SOCIAL AND MORAL CONDITIONS under Negroes and HISTORY AND CONDITION under women. Only Blacks had both a social *and* a moral condition; only women had both a history *and* a condition. Not so clear, however, is the subtle reinforcement of the majority assumptions provided by such subdivisions as CIVILIZATION OF under the names of indigenous American and African peoples, DISCOVERY AND EXPLORATION under geographic names, and the description of encounters between indigenous and colonizing peoples as MASSACRES when the indigenous people won and BATTLES when the colonists won.

The use of the first of these three subdivisions denies the fact that many indigenous peoples had highly developed civilizations, albeit that the form of their civilization may not have been recognized (or acknowledged, if recognized, since it was not Western) by the colonizing people. The second subdivision reinforces the notion, popularly held by Americans and Western Europeans, that the world outside of Western Europe had no history—and only a shaky hold on existence—before it was "discovered" by Western Europeans (which further reinforces the notion that Western Europeans "civilized" the world in the best interests of us all).

These subdivisions could be neutralized by changing CIVILIZATION OF to RELATIONS WITH [COLONIZING PEOPLE] and by requiring that DISCOVERY AND EXPLORATION be modified to specify who did the discovering; for example, AMERICA—DISCOVERY AND EXPLORATION, SPANISH.

The use of the term massacre was defended by Eugene Frosio, LC's Principal Subject Cataloger: "Events are not named according to what it is polite or ideal to call them, but according to what they are actually called by authorities in the field."[3] The authority Frosio cites is the *Encyclopaedia Britannica*. Had he consulted an Indian history, he would have found, for instance, that what the *Britannica* calls the Fort Phil Kearney massacre the Indians call the Battle of the Hundred Slain.[4]

Whether an encounter between an indigenous and a colonizing people was a battle or a massacre is, more often than not, determined by who is writing the history rather than by any objective facts. Massacre is a value-loaded word and should be avoided. If the word battle does not appropriately describe an armed encounter between peoples, the neutral word incident should be used. (The use of the word incident was suggested by Thomas Yen-Ran Yeh; it was Yen-Ran Yeh's suggestion that led to Frosio's response.[5])

3. The wording and structure of headings for minority or other groups should not differ from headings for the majority. Avoid all *as* and *in* constructions to describe practitioners of an activity.

The much-criticized DELINQUENT WOMEN was changed to FEMALE OFFENDERS in 1974. This is the term in current usage in the criminal justice literature, and it certainly is an improvement over the old heading, but it is not in line with other headings for criminals. Was FEMALE OFFENDERS established because of literary warrant or because one would not logically send "true" criminals to REFORMATORIES FOR WOMEN (the *LCSH* heading) rather than to prison?

But the question of whether women are delinquent, offenders, or criminals aside, we are still left with the fact that four, and only four, classes of persons are singled out in the *LCSH* as criminals. Why do only Catholics, Jews, Blacks, and women transcend their particular nationality? The other criminal elements in society are supposedly adequately described by the heading CRIME AND CRIMINALS—[GEOGRAPHIC SUBDIVISION]. This heading is not comparable to the adjectival heading. The adjectival heading is valid and provides valuable access, but it should be applied to all classes of people and to all nationalities or to none. (See the thesaurus for a suggested restructuring of access points.)

The *as* form, WOMEN AS LIBRARIANS for instance, has been abandoned by LC under women; it persists in other entries in the *LCSH* (GURKHAS AS SOLDIERS for instance). The *in* form also persists although the arguments against its use are the arguments against the *as* form. Its use connotes peculiarity (the people so described are acting out a somewhat inappropriate role) and passiveness (they are not actively participating in that role). "Women in librarianship" would have been viewed by women librarians as equally inaccurate and offensive as the abandoned *LCSH* form.

The use of the *in* form, in addition to all of its other faults, is also potentially confusing to a library user. The distinction between WOMEN IN ISLAM and WOMEN, MUSLIM would be moot to all but a few fairly sophisticated library users. The heading for Islamic theological works on woman should be constructed in the same way that Islamic theological works on man are constructed.

4. Be specific and current. Do not use previously established terms to cover new topics.

Haykin's guideline concerning specificity is: "The heading should be as specific as the topic it is intended to cover. As a corollary, the heading should not be broader than the topic; rather than use a broader heading, the cataloger should use two specific headings which will approximately cover it."[6] LC's policy (as determined from an examination of their cataloging) in assigning subject headings to materials on women and minorities is to ignore Haykin's basic caveat and to apply his escape clause.

Works, for instance, on the employment of African-American women are given two headings, neither of which is specific: WOMEN—EMPLOYMENT—UNITED STATES and NEGRO WOMEN. A user must look through one or the other of the files (both of which are huge because of the nonspecificity of their application) and match tracings to find works on the subject. This requirement for access places the onus on the user, who must be both dedicated to the search and fairly sophisticated.

While there is certainly justification for not establishing a subject heading, or a subdivision of an existing heading, on the basis of one title (and, therefore, applying Haykin's escape clause and assigning two headings which approach specificity to a work), there is hardly justification for continuing this practice when hundreds of titles are involved.

A few specific examples of LC nonspecificity: Kelly Hamilton's *Goals and plans of Black women; a sociological study* (1975; cataloged 1975) was assigned NEGROES—EDUCATION, WOMEN, NEGRO, and EDUCATION OF WOMEN. The fact that none of the headings specifically relates education and Black women is only half the problem. The work is actually a study of the effects of attending a predominantly Black or a racially integrated university (*higher* education) on the levels of achievement orientation and educational aspirations expressed by Black women students.

Phyllis Ann Wallace's *Pathways to work: unemployment among Black teenage females* (1974; cataloged 1974) was assigned YOUTH—EMPLOYMENT—NEW YORK (CITY), NEGRO YOUTH—EMPLOYMENT, and WOMEN, NEGRO.

William Mandel's *Soviet women* (1975; cataloged 1974) was assigned WOMEN—RUSSIA and WOMEN—HISTORY. Mandel's work is a history of women's status in the U.S.S.R. The first heading is nonspecific; it should have been WOMEN—RUSSIA (even better, U.S.S.R.)—SOCIAL CONDITIONS—1917– . The second heading is simply ridiculous! It serves no purpose but to swell the file and make it near impossible to find general histories of women. Women are not universals; we are rooted in a place and in a time.

Women and ACES; perspectives and issues (1974; cataloged 1974) was assigned COUNSELING AS A PROFESSION (this would now be COUNSELING—VOCATIONAL GUIDANCE due to a recent *LCSH* revision), SEX DISCRIMINATION, and COUNSELING—STUDY AND TEACHING. The introduction to the work states: ''The purpose of this monograph is to inform ACES membership on (1) the status of women in counseling, and (2) the status of the counseling education program regarding training procedures in counseling females'' (p. v). The stated purpose of the work is not brought out in the tracings. Why isn't there, at the very least and even though it would be nonspecific, a heading for WOMEN COUNSELORS.

Currency and specificity are two sides of the same coin. If subject heading terms are not current, they are not specific. LC didn't establish SEX DISCRIMINATION until 1974. At that time they also established SEX DISCRIMINATION AGAINST WOMEN and SEX DISCRIMINATION IN EDUCATION. They still have not established a heading for affirmative action. And even though the sex discrimination headings were so recently established, the run of cards under the headings has assumed considerable proportions since the various forms that sex discrimination can take (e.g. in consumer credit, in housing, in public accommodations, in employment, etc.) are all entered simply under SEX DISCRIMINATION or SEX DISCRIMINATION AGAINST WOMEN.

Specificity is also achieved through the liberal use of general subdivisions. The *LCSH* heading WOMEN IN TRADE-UNIONS, for instance, should have been subdivided, considering the titles entered under the heading, by BIOGRAPHY, HISTORY, and PERSONAL NARRATIVES; it should also be subdivided geographically. (In addition, a specific heading for sex discrimination in labor unions is needed.) Had these subdivisions been applied, a user interested in the history of women labor unionists in Great Britain would not have to go through the entire file to find the material wanted, and the user interested in everything in the collection on women labor unionists would still have access.

5. Do not use subsuming terminology. Do not establish headings for some, but not all, classes of people or peoples.

Subsuming terminology and the selective establishment of headings for some, but not all, classes of people also violate Haykin's guideline concerning specificity. These types of headings, in addition to exhibiting a bias in favor of the *LCSH* hypothetical user, actively disserve the user.

Headings such as PILGRIM FATHERS and FIREMEN, since they are assigned to works on both men and women Pilgrims and fire fighters, are not specific. Tradition may sanction the use of man to mean humankind; it does not sanction subsuming Pilgrim women under Pilgrim men. PILGRIMS (NEW ENGLAND SETTLERS) and FIRE FIGHTERS would be specific, and the user would not have to intuit that these headings perhaps covered the activities of women as well as of men. If literary warrant dictates, the headings PILGRIM MEN and PILGRIM WOMEN, FIREMEN and FIREWOMEN (with appropriate references from and to the general term) should be established.

Headings such as SPORTS FOR WOMEN and SPORTS FOR CHILDREN are specific, but there is no heading for men's sports. Hence, the basic heading, SPORTS, is used both as a heading broader than the topic covered (when it is applied to works on sports for men) and as a specific heading (when it is applied to works on sports for all ages and sexes). The user interested in children's sports is obliged to differentiate between those works which are general and those which are on men's sports when looking under the general heading. The user interested in men's sports has the same difficulty. The heading SPORTS should be assigned only to general works; a heading, SPORTS FOR MEN, should be established.

I can find only one instance in all of the 2,026 pages of the *LCSH* of the establishment of a discrete heading for men, to parallel those established for women, children, etc., under a topic. There is a heading for SEX INSTRUCTION FOR MEN. If catalogers can distinguish between general works on sex instruction and works on sex instruction for men, women, boys, girls, etc., they should be able to do the same for works on sports, self-defense, gymnastics, and all of the other topics for which the *LCSH* subject heading pattern follows that of SPORTS rather than that of SEX INSTRUCTION.

6. Do not allow huge files of undifferentiated cards to accumulate under a heading. One inch of cards represents approximately 100 titles; it takes quite some time and patience on the part of a user to examine that many titles in order to select those wanted.

The use of specific headings and of general subdivisions reduces the likelihood of building up huge files. But a rule of thumb is needed which would require that a subject heading be reexamined for its specificity, or possible subdivision, after it has been assigned to a specified number of titles. Had LC such a rule, the mass of cards under WOMEN—EMPLOYMENT, for instance, (which includes works on opportunities for employment, the health and safety hazards of employment, the wages of employment, discrimination in employment, the problems of mothers, married and/or single women and employment, employment statistics, women in professional, business, trade, and home employment, reentry into employment, the history of women's employment, and employment law) might not have accumulated.

My suggestion for a rule of thumb is one card more than an average thumb, or about two inches of cards. This would mean that if a heading had been assigned approximately 200 times, it would be examined for specificity and/or the addition of subdivision. If the heading is specific, and if no general subdivisions are applicable to the topic, the heading should be subdivided by date of publication if date of publication subdivision is reasonable.

References:

1. Haykin, David Judson. *Subject headings; a practical guide.* U.S. Government Printing Office, 1951. p. 7.
2. *Ibid.,* p. 7.
3. Frosio, Eugene. In *Library resources and technical services,* Spring 1971, p. 131.
4. Brown, Dee. *Bury my heart at Wounded Knee.* Bantam, 1972. p. 132.
5. Yen-Ran Yeh, Thomas. In *Library resources and technical services,* Spring 1971, p. 122–28.
6. Haykin, *op. cit.,* p. 9.

How to Use the Thesaurus

General Considerations

Audience

The thesaurus is designed for use in analyzing book and periodical collections and for use in indexing the contents of books and periodicals. The structure of the list makes it possible to select the level of specificity desirable in the particular library environment. For example, a work on sex discrimination might include chapters on sex discrimination in consumer credit, in education, in employment, and in public accommodations. The BT-NT structure of the list will lead the person assigning a subject heading to the work from the four specific terms (NT's) to the broader term (BT), SEX DISCRIMINATION. The broader term should be assigned to such a work if full content analysis (the assignment of all four of the specific terms) is not felt to be desirable. If the four specific terms are assigned, the broader term is no longer specific and should not be assigned.

In assigning subject headings, two questions to ask are: Is the descriptor neither broader nor narrower than the topic? Is there a special aspect of the work, even if covered by the descriptor, that should be brought out? If the hypothetical work on sex discrimination were being added to a collection that had a special subject emphasis (e.g. a feminist credit union's library), the broader term and the specific term that represented the particular interest of the users of that collection, SEX DISCRIMINATION IN CONSUMER CREDIT, might both be assigned. Or, a work on the socialization of women might include a bibliography on sexism in children's literature. Is this an aspect of the work that needs to be brought out?

Users of the thesaurus must determine for themselves the level of specificity desirable. One might establish, as a guideline, a maximum number of specific headings to be assigned any work; if a work requires more specific headings than the maximum allowable, use a broader term or terms. Of course, there will have to be exceptions (there always are!).

Direct vs. indirect entry under terms

It was the decision of the Committee on Sexism in Subject Headings to limit direct entry under the term women whenever possible and practical. This decision was based on two considerations. The first was our belief that indirect entry has a consciousness-raising value. The user of the catalog interested in works on photographers—and who has, consciously or subconsciously, white, male photographers in mind—will find at the access point for photographers the general heading and headings for PHOTOGRAPHERS, AFRICAN-AMERICAN, PHOTOGRAPHERS, MEN, and PHOTOGRAPHERS, WOMEN.

The second consideration was our belief that the practice of direct entry is at least partially responsible for the paucity of subject analysis given to works of concern to women and minorities. If women is considered a true subject term, rather than a modifier of a topical subject heading, the cataloger is likely to feel that a major part of the analysis of a work has been completed once it has been determined that a work is about women.

All occupational headings in the thesaurus are in inverted form. Many topical headings are established in phrase form so that general works on the topic and works on women are kept together in the catalog; for example, AFFIRMATIVE ACTION FOR WOMEN, ORDINATION OF WOMEN, SPORTS FOR WOMEN.

Direct access under women has been retained in those instances where inversion would not have accomplished our consciousness-raising end and might have resulted in a complex file. The use of EDUCATION—WOMEN rather than WOMEN—EDUCATION still would result in all the materials on women's education being segregated at one point in the file. And that point would be somewhere between EDUCATION—WISCONSIN and EDUCATION—WYOMING.

The entries filed under EDUCATION—WOMEN could be dispersed throughout the file under the basic term by interposing the subdivisions used under EDUCATION between the two terms. The resulting file would hinder access to materials on women's education and would, on occasion, result in ambiguous headings; for example:

Education (Indirect)
Education—Attitudes of teachers
Education—Attitudes of teachers—Women
Education—Counseling
Education—Counseling—Women
Education—Curricula
Education—Curricula, Nonsexist
Education—Great Britain
Education—Great Britain—Women
Education—Role conflict—Women
Education—United States
Education—United States—Women

It would be difficult to gain ready access to relevant materials in such a file, and the cross-references needed to provide any access would swell the size of the file. The third and the tenth headings are also much less ambiguous when they are established as WOMEN—EDUCATION—ATTITUDES OF TEACHERS and WOMEN—EDUCATION—ROLE CONFLICT.

Direct access has been retained also for some headings that could have been inverted or subdivided. In instances where the provision of access to general works on a topic and works specifically on or for women was not needed nor desirable, direct access was retained; for example, WOMEN—LIBRARY RESOURCES was retained since a user interested in the topic would not be served by works listed under the general term.

Terms included and terms excluded

The terms listed are of three types: (1) additions to the *LCSH* to cover areas of women's concerns that are not presently covered; (2) revisions of biased *LCSH* terms; and (3) *LCSH* headings which have been included merely to expand the reference structure or to add subdivisions. In relation to type three, *LCSH* headings which were included for this reason may have additional *LCSH* references and subdivisions which have not been included. These additional references and subdivisions are not being recommended for deletion from the *LCSH*. Their inclusion was not relevant to the intent of the list, which is to provide both a list of descriptors suitable for indexing materials of concern to women and other classes of people who have not been well served by the *LCSH* and a critique of the *LCSH* and LC's subject heading assignment policies.

The terms included in the thesaurus, and each term's related reference structure, are models. Occupational headings, for example, should be constructed on the models of ATHLETICS COACHES, WOMEN or BUSINESSWOMEN, as appropriate. WOMAN (CHRISTIAN THEOLOGY) and WOMAN (JEWISH THEOLOGY), and their related terms and references, are models for all theology/religion headings relating to women. (Both Christianity and Judaism were included only because of recommended changes in related *LCSH* headings.)

The subdivision structure under specific headings is also to be used as a model. Subdivisions established under, for example, WOMEN, WOMEN—EDUCATION, and WOMEN—EMPLOYMENT are to be used under GIRLS, TEEN AGE WOMEN, MIDDLE AGE WOMEN, SENIOR WOMEN, AFRICAN-AMERICAN WOMEN, etc., as appropriate. The display of headings under the term AUTHORS is a model.

SEX DISCRIMINATION, REVERSE SEX DISCRIMINATION, SEXISM, NONSEXIST, and FEMINIST are all listed as terms, or as subdivisions or modifiers of terms, in the thesaurus. The literature, if the rule of specificity is to be adhered to, requires this proliferation of terms. In assigning these headings to works, as in assigning any subject descriptor to any work, the cataloger must be guided by the author's intent. SEX DISCRIMINATION and REVERSE SEX DISCRIMINATION should be assigned to works on overt and legally prohibited discrimination against women or men based solely upon sex (e.g. to a work on discriminatory child care leave practices). SEXISM should be assigned to works on the conscious or unconscious oppression of women because of their sex (e.g. to a work on how academic counselors "track" women students out of certain professions and into others). NONSEXIST should be assigned to works on conscious attempts to identify and eliminate sexism (e.g. to a work on how to write nonsexist textbooks). FEMINIST should be assigned to works with a professed feminist orientation (e.g. to a work on a feminist reinterpretation of human evolution).

The thesaurus does *not* include headings for men to parallel those recommended for women in every instance. Such headings are implicit wherever they would be appropriate.

Form and topical subdivisions

The terms in the thesaurus may be subdivided by topic and/or by form. Topical subdivisions expand the scope of the heading (e.g. WOMEN—EMPLOYMENT—SEX ROLE CONFLICT). EMPLOYMENT and SEX ROLE CONFLICT are both topical subdivisions. Form subdivisions specify the form of the material (e.g. BIOGRAPHY, CONGRESSES, PERIODICALS).

Most of the subdivisions used in the thesaurus are standard *LCSH* subdivisions (e.g. ECONOMIC CONDITIONS, HISTORY, LEGAL STATUS, LAWS, ETC.,

SOCIAL CONDITIONS). In order to improve access, the following subdivisions (which are not used or are used differently in the *LCSH*) were established.

Feminist perspective. This subdivision is topical; it may be used to subdivide or further subdivide any topic.

JUDAEO-CHRISTIAN RELIGIOUS TRADITION—FEMINIST PERSPECTIVE, for example, should be assigned to works such as: Ruether, Rosemary Radford, *Religion and sexism; images of women in the Jewish and Christian tradition* (1974), which attempts to present "a more exact idea of the role of [the Judaeo-Christian traditional] religion in shaping traditional cultural images that have degraded and suppressed women"; *Christian freedom for women and other human beings* (1975); and Swidler, Leonard, "Jesus was a feminist," *The Catholic world,* January 1971.

CHILD CARE—FEMINIST PERSPECTIVE should be assigned to works such as Task Force on Working Women, *Exploitation from 9 to 5* (1975): "The lack of good, reasonably priced and convenient child care is a major barrier to equal rights for women." "Child care is a complex issue, but without child care, the right of women to work will not be a reality. . . . It should be clear, however, that custodial child care is not what parents and children want. Child care should, by now, be synonymous with an educational experience."

Law and legislation. This subdivision is a form; it may be used to subdivide or further subdivide any topic.

In *LCSH* this subdivision is used as both a form and a topical subdivision. For example, editions of laws on employment and discussions of laws on employment are both supposed to be assigned the heading EMPLOYMENT—LAW AND LEGISLATION. Even if LC applied the subdivision consistently (which it does not), the confusion that results from the lack of specificity impedes access. In the thesaurus, LAW AND LEGISLATION has been used only as a form subdivision; LEGAL ASPECTS has been established as a topical subdivision.

Legal aspects. This subdivision is topical; it may be used to subdivide or further subdivide any topic.

In the thesaurus it has been used, for example, under ABORTION for works about abortion law and legislation and for guides to the law designed for the lay person.

Popular works. This subdivision is a form; it may be used to subdivide or further subdivide any technical subject.

POPULAR WORKS is an *LCSH* subdivision. An examination of their catalog, however, revealed that LC did not apply the subdivision freely enough under headings such as GYNECOLOGY and OBSTETRICS. The free application of the subdivision is recommended in libraries which collect works in these areas for both the specialist and the lay person.

The use of the subdivision is not recommended in general libraries which collect works primarily for lay persons since it might create a bias against the material as nonauthoritative.

Status. This subdivision is topical; it may be used to subdivide any occupational heading.

In the thesaurus this subdivision has been used, for example, under the headings for ATHLETICS COACHES, WOMEN and BUSINESSWOMEN for works on the status of women in those occupations.

Geographic subdivision

The matter of how and where to geographically subdivide any subject descriptor presents a number of problems; the form and the placement of the geographic subdivision affect the shape of the file and the access it provides.

The form of the subdivision—using *LCSH* terminology—can be *direct* (e.g. a work relating to Chicago is subdivided by CHICAGO) or *indirect* (e.g. a work relating to Chicago is subdivided by UNITED STATES—ILLINOIS—CHICAGO or ILLINOIS—CHICAGO). LC's current policy on geographic subdivision is to subdivide indirectly; the name of the relevant-country is interposed between the heading and any subordinate political, administrative, or geographical division within the country; e.g. a work on women in Geneva would be entered under WOMEN—SWITZERLAND—GENEVA. LC does, however, make an exception to this form of indirect subdivision for the states, provinces, constituent countries, or territories of the United States, Canada, and Great Britain; e.g. WOMEN—CALIFORNIA—LOS ANGELES rather than WOMEN—UNITED STATES—CALIFORNIA—LOS ANGELES, WOMEN—MANITOBA—WINNIPEG rather than WOMEN—CANADA—MANITOBA—WINNIPEG.

The use of the exception is not recommended. The use of the exception makes it difficult to locate the full extent of materials available on a given topic in a given country. A user interested, for instance, in women's employment in Canada would have to search under 12 places in the file (i.e. WOMEN—EMPLOYMENT—CANADA, WOMEN—EMPLOYMENT—BRITISH COLUMBIA, WOMEN—EMPLOYMENT—NOVA SCOTIA, etc.—some of these searches, inevitably, will be fruitless); these 12 headings will be interfiled with headings for WOMEN —EMPLOYMENT—FRANCE, WOMEN—EMPLOYMENT —NEW YORK (STATE), etc. A user interested in women's employment in the United States would have to search under 51 places in the file.

Interposing the name of the country provides direct access to materials for those users interested in, at least, being aware of everything in the collection, and it does not hinder access to those users whose interests are restricted to a limited geographical locale; the user interested only in women's employment in Winnipeg would not be hindered if the entry were WOMEN—EMPLOYMENT— CANADA—MANITOBA—WINNIPEG providing that appropriate cross references were established from WOMEN—EMPLOYMENT—MANITOBA and WOMEN— EMPLOYMENT—WINNIPEG. (The second reference would be necessary even if the LC exception to indirect subdivision is accepted.)

If the collection being indexed is limited to works about one country, region, etc., the interposition of the country or region is unnecessary. For example, if a collection is limited to works on the United States, the interposition of United States before Alabama is irrelevant. The question is, should Alabama be interposed before Mobile?

The placement of the geographic subdivision, whatever its form, also affects the shape of the file and the access it provides. The decision of where to place a geographic subdivision should be based on the scope of the collection and on the projected users of the collection. For example, if the decision is to subdivide the term WOMEN geographically without exception, the file will keep all works on women in a given place together, but it will separate works on the same topic in various places:

Women (Indirect) [i.e. the geographic subdivision precedes any other subdivision]
Women—Civil rights
Women—Education
Women—Employment
Women—Great Britain
Women—Great Britain—Civil rights
Women—Great Britain—Education
Women—Great Britain—Employment
Women—Great Britain—Legal status, laws, etc.
Women—Great Britain—Personal conduct, life styles, etc.
Women—Great Britain—Songs and Music
Women—Legal status, laws, etc.
Women—Personal conduct, lifestyles, etc.
Women—Songs and music
Women—United States
Women—United States—Civil rights [Education, etc. as under Great Britain above]

If in addition to subdividing the term WOMEN geographically, the decision is to keep certain top-

ics together by subdividing the topic geographically, the resulting file might be:

Women (Indirect)
Women—Civil rights (Indirect)
Women—Civil rights—Great Britain
Women—Civil rights—United States
Women—Education (Indirect)
Women—Education—Great Britain
Women—Education—United States
Women—Employment (Indirect)
Women—Employment—Great Britain
Women—Employment—United States
Women—Great Britain
Women—Great Britain—Personal conduct, lifestyles, etc.
Women—Great Britain—Songs and music
Women—Legal status, laws, etc. (Indirect)
Women—Legal status, laws, etc.—Great Britain
Women—Legal status, laws, etc.—United States.
Women—Personal conduct, lifestyles, etc.
Women—Songs and music
Women—United States
Women—United States—Personal conduct, lifestyles, etc.
Women—United States—Songs and music

If the decision is to keep all works about women in a given place together, narrower term references should be made under the general term; e.g. if the entry is to be WOMEN—GREAT BRITAIN— EMPLOYMENT, either specific narrower term references, or a narrower term note (NT WOMEN— GREAT BRITAIN—EMPLOYMENT; WOMEN—UNITED STATES—EMPLOYMENT and similar headings), should be set up under WOMEN—EMPLOYMENT.

If the decision is to keep certain topics together, narrower term references should be made under the general term for the place; e.g. if the entry is to be WOMEN—EMPLOYMENT—GREAT BRIT- AIN, either specific narrower term references, or a narrower term note (NT WOMEN—EMPLOYMENT— GREAT BRITAIN; WOMEN—LEGAL STATUS, LAWS, ETC. —GREAT BRITAIN and similar headings), should be set up under WOMEN—GREAT BRITAIN.

Since the thesaurus is a collection of models and has not been developed with the indexing requirements of any particular collection in mind, I have not given general instructions for geographic subdivision. I have, however, subdivided geographically in a few instances so that I could provide model headings and their related reference structure. For example, I have indicated that WOM- EN—EMPLOYMENT is to be subdivided geographically; this permitted me to establish:

Women—Employment—United States
  NT   Minority women—Employment—United States

Minority women—Employment (Indirect)
  BT   Women—Employment

Minority women—Employment—United States
  BT   Women—Employment—United States
  NT   African-American women—Employment

Organization

Filing order

  TERM (e.g. ABORTION)
  TERM—SUBDIVISION (e.g. ABORTION—PSY-
CHOLOGICAL ASPECTS; subdivisions are used to limit
the scope of basic terms)
  TERM (GLOSS) (e.g. ABSENCE, LEAVE OF (EMPLOY-
MENT); glosses are used to limit the scope of terms
which might be ambiguous)
  TERM, MODIFIER (e.g. AUTHORS, WOMEN; normal
word order terms which have been inverted are
used to bring related materials together and/or to
bring the probable point of direct user access into
primary position)
  TERM [AS THE BEGINNING OF A PHRASE] (e.g. CHIL-
DREN OF DIVORCED PARENTS; phrase headings are
used when it is necessary to define the relationship
of one term to another)

Reference structure

The thesaurus is organized in accordance with
the American National Standards Institute's
*Guidelines for thesaurus structure, construction,
and use* (ANSI Z39.19-1974).

Cross references. The following relationships
between and among terms are shown under entry
term:
(1) The term's place in the hierarchy (i.e. whether it is
broader than certain terms and narrower than others).
(2) The term's nonhierarchical relationship to other
terms.
(3) Terms which could have substituted for the term
chosen as the entry term (i.e. synonyms).

For example:

Interpersonal relations, Nonsexist		Entry term
BT	Interpersonal relations	Broader term
RT	Sexism in interpersonal relations	Related term
NT	Interpersonal relations in marriage, Nonsexist	Narrower term
UF	Nonsexist interpersonal relations	Term not used as entry term (Use for)

Each term identified as a broader term (BT)
must have a reciprocal narrower term (NT) which
appears in the list as a heading. Each term identified
as a related term (RT) must have a reciprocal related term (RT) which appears in the list as a heading. Each term identified as a use for term (UF)
must have a reciprocal USE term which appears in
the list as a reference. The example above would
generate the following reciprocal terms:

Interpersonal relations		Entry term
NT	Interpersonal relations, Nonsexist	Narrower term
	Sexism in interpersonal relations	Narrower term

Sexism in interpersonal relations		Entry term
BT	Interpersonal relations	Broader term
RT	Interpersonal relations, Nonsexist	Related term

Interpersonal relations in marriage, Nonsexist		Entry term
BT	Interpersonal relations, Nonsexist	

Nonsexist interpersonal relations	
USE	Interpersonal relations, Nonsexist

Notes. There are three types of notes that are
actually part of the structure of the thesaurus: *here
are entered* notes, *cf.* notes, and related heading
notes.

Here are entered notes describe the scope of
the entry term and often refer the user to related
terms. For example:

Married women—Legal status, laws, etc.
Here are entered works on the effect of
marriage on women's legal capacity. Works on
legal relations between husband and wife are
entered under HUSBAND AND WIFE. Works on the
legal status of women in general are entered
under WOMEN—LEGAL STATUS, LAWS, ETC.

Cf. notes refer the user of the thesaurus to full
here are entered notes; for example:

Homosexual men in literature
cf. note under HOMOSEXUALS IN LITERATURE

These notes should be converted to full *here
are entered* notes in a public catalog; for example:

Homosexual men in literature
Here are entered works on the representation
of homosexual men in literature. Works on
homosexual men authors are entered under
AUTHORS, HOMOSEXUAL MEN.

Related heading notes refer the user to classes
of related or narrower headings; for example:

Lesbians
  RT   headings beginning with the words
      LESBIAN and LESBIANS

Human resources policy—Feminist perspective
NT   subdivision FEMINIST PERSPECTIVE under
CHILD CARE, PART-TIME EMPLOYMENT
and similar headings; also
subdivision HUMAN RESOURCES
POLICY—FEMINIST PERSPECTIVE under
names of countries, regions, cities,
etc.

There are two types of marginal notes that are not part of the structure of the thesaurus. The first type identifies the entry term's relationship to the *LCSH*. All *LCSH* headings are identified by an LC in the left margin opposite the term. All substitutions for established *LCSH* terms are identified in the right margin; for example:

Criminals, women   *LCSH:* Female offenders

The second type of marginal note is a miscellany. These notes supplement the introduction to the thesaurus. They include justifications for the establishment of headings by means of literature citations, explanations of LC subject cataloging practice, and occasional diatribes.

Part Two

Thesaurus for Nonsexist Indexing and Cataloging

Abandonment of family
  USE   Desertion and nonsupport

LC **Abolitionists**
      BT   Slavery in the United States

Abolitionists, Women
      BT   Slavery in the United States—Anti-slavery movements—Women's
              activities
              Women—United States—Biography
      UF   Women abolitionists

LC **Abortion**
      BT   Birth control
              Obstetrics
              Pregnancy
      RT   Miscarriage
      UF   Induced abortion
              Intentional abortion

In the LCSH UF references are made from the terms Feticide *and* Miscarriage. *In this list* Miscarriage *is an entry term.* Feticide, *even as a UF reference, and the LCSH RT references from* Infanticide *and* Offenses against the person *should be dropped; these references imply a point of view concerning abortion which is not universally agreed upon.*

LC **Abortion—Law and legislation**
    Here are entered annotated and unannotated editions of the law and
    legislation governing abortion. Works about abortion law and legislation
    and guides to the law designed for the lay person are entered under
    ABORTION—LEGAL ASPECTS.
      BT   Sex and law
      RT   Abortion—Legal aspects
              Right to life movement

Abortion—Legal aspects
      RT   Abortion—Law and legislation; cf. note under ABORTION—LAW
                      AND LEGISLATION

LC **Abortion—Psychological aspects**
      RT   Abortion clinics and referral services
              Abortion counseling
              Pregnancy—Psychological aspects

Abortion, Spontaneous
  USE   Miscarriage

Abortion clinics and referral services
      BT   Women's projects and services
      RT   Abortion—Psychological aspects
              Abortion counseling
      UF   Abortion referral services

Abortion counseling
      BT   Counseling for women
      RT   Abortion—Psychological aspects
              Abortion clinics and referral services
              Pregnancy counseling

Abortion referral services
  USE   Abortion clinics and referral services

Absence, Leave of (Employment)
  USE   Leave of absence (Employment)

LC **Absenteeism (Labor)**
      BT   Job satisfaction
              Alienation (Social psychology)
      UF   Employee absenteeism
              Labor absenteeism

Absenteeism (Labor)—Women
      RT   Child care
              Women—Employment—Job satisfaction
      UF   Women—Employment—Absenteeism

LC **Achievement motivation**
      NT   Achievement motivation and sex role

Achievement motivation and sex role
      BT   Achievement motivation
      RT   Sex role conflict

Achievement motivation and sex role (cont.)
   NT   Achievement motivation and sex role of men
          Achievement motivation and sex role of women
   UF   Sex role and achievement motivation

Achievement motivation and sex role of men
   BT   Achievement motivation and sex role
   UF   Men—Achievement motivation and sex role
          Men—Sex role and achievement motivation

Achievement motivation and sex role of women
   BT   Achievement motivation and sex role
   UF   Women—Achievement motivation and sex role
          Women—Sex role and achievement motivation

Academic counseling, Nonsexist
   BT   Academic counseling for women
   RT   Sexism in academic counseling
          Women—Education—Role conflict
   UF   Men—Education—Nonsexist counseling
          Women—Education—Nonsexist counseling

Academic counseling for women
   BT   Counseling for women
   NT   Academic counseling, Nonsexist
   UF   Women—Academic counseling
          Women—Education—Counseling

Actors and actresses   *LCSH:* Actors
   UF   Actresses and actors

Actors and actresses, Homosexual
   UF   Homosexual actors and actresses

Actresses and actors
  USE   Actors and actresses

Adolescence
  USE   Teen age

Adopted children
  USE   Children, Adopted

LC **Adoption**
   BT   Family planning
          Parent and child (Law)
   RT   Children, Adopted
   NT   Interadoption
   UF   Child adoption
          Child placing

Adoption, Interethnic
  USE   Interethnic adoption

Adoption, Interfaith
  USE   Interreligious adoption

Adoption, International
  USE   International adoption

Adoption, Interracial
  USE   Interracial adoption

Adoption, Interreligious
  USE   Interreligious adoption

Adoption, Mixed
  USE   Interadoption

Adoption, One-parent
  USE   Single-parent adoption

Adoption, Single-parent
  USE   Single-parent adoption

Adoption, Transethnic
  USE   Interethnic adoption

Adoption, Transracial
　USE　Interracial adoption

LC **Adult education**
　BT　Education
　UF　Adults, Education of
　　　Continuing education
　　　Education, Continuing
　　　Education of adults
　　　Lifelong education

Adult education—Women
　USE　Women—Adult education

Adultery
Here are entered general religious works on adultery as a sin and/or as a
civil crime. General works on extramarital sexual relations are entered
under EXTRAMARITAL RELATIONS.
　BT　Extramarital relations

Adults, Education of
　USE　Adult education

Advertising, Nonsexist
　BT　Mass media, Nonsexist
　RT　Sexism in advertising
　UF　Nonsexist advertising

Advertising, Sexism in
　USE　Sexism in advertising

"Affairs" (Amorous relationships)
　USE　Extramarital relations

Affirmative action
Here are entered works on model or actual affirmative action plans and
programs, and general descriptions of the effect of both federal and state
affirmative action laws relating to equal employment opportunity. The laws
are entered under DISCRIMINATION IN EMPLOYMENT—LAW AND LEGISLATION.
　BT　Civil rights
　RT　Discrimination in employment—Law and legislation
　NT　Affirmative action for women

Affirmative action for women
Here are entered works on model or actual affirmative action plans and
programs affecting women's employment, and general descriptions of the
effect of both federal and state affirmative action laws relating to equal
employment opportunity for women. The laws are entered under SEX
DISCRIMINATION IN EMPLOYMENT—LAW AND LEGISLATION. General works on
laws affecting women's employment which are not limited to affirmative
action law are entered under WOMEN—EMPLOYMENT—LEGAL ASPECTS
　BT　Affirmative action
　　　Labor laws and legislation—Women
　　　Women—Civil rights
　RT　Affirmative action organizations, centers, etc.
　　　Sex discrimination in employment—Law and legislation
　　　Women—Employment—Legal aspects
　UF　Women—Affirmative action
　　　Women, Affirmative action for

Affirmative action organizations, centers, etc.
　BT　Women's projects and services
　RT　Affirmative action for women
　　　Employment agencies
　　　Job hunting for women

African-American girls
　BT　African-American women
　UF　Afro-Americans
　　　Black Americans
　　　Blacks—United States
　　　Negroes—United States

LCSH: Afro-American . . . *The LCSH
form was rejected on the basis of arguments from analogy; Italo-American is
not used for Italian-American, Mex-
American is not used for Mexican
American, As-American is not used for*

African-American women
   BT   African-Americans
            Minority women—United States
   NT   African-American girls
   UF   Afro-Americans
            Black Americans
            Blacks—United States
            Negroes—United States

African-American women—Education
   BT   Minority women—Education—United States

African-American women—Employment
   BT   Minority women—Employment—United States

African-American women students—Aspirations
   USE   Student aspirations—African-American women

African-American women's organizations
   BT   Women's organizations—United States

African-Americans
   NT   African-American women
   UF   Afro-Americans
            Black Americans
            Blacks—United States
            Negroes—United States

Afro-Americans
   USE   African-Americans; and AFRICAN-AMERICAN WOMEN, AFRICAN-
               AMERICAN GIRLS, etc.

LC **Age and employment**
Here are entered works on age as a factor in finding and keeping suitable
employment.
   RT   Age discrimination in employment
   NT   Middle age and employment
            Seniors and employment
            Teen age and employment
   UF   Employment and age

Age and employment—Women
   BT   Women—Employment

Age discrimination
Here are entered works on discrimination based on age.
   BT   Discrimination
   NT   Age discrimination in employment
   UF   Ageism

Age discrimination in employment
   BT   Age discrimination
            Discrimination in employment
   RT   Age and employment
   UF   Employment, Age discrimination in

Age discrimination in employment—Women
   BT   Women—Employment
   RT   Sex discrimination in employment

The aged
   USE   Seniors

Ageism
   USE   Age discrimination

Agencies, Employment
   USE   Employment agencies

LC **Aggressiveness (Psychology)**
   BT   Psychology
   RT   Assertiveness (Psychology)
            Violence

Aggressiveness (Psychology) in Women
   BT   Sex role socialization of women
            Women—Psychology

*Asian-American, etc. And, as Black
women of my acquaintance insist,
"Afro" is a hairdo.*

    UF   Women—Aggressiveness

Agricultural laborers
  USE   Agricultural workers

Agricultural workers
    BT   Working classes—Employment
    NT   Agricultural workers, Women
    UF   Agricultural laborers
           Farm laborers
           Farm workers
           Farmworkers
           Workers, Agricultural
           Workers, Farm

Agricultural workers, Women
    BT   Agricultural workers
           Working class women—Employment
    UF   Women agricultural workers
           Women farm workers
           Women farmworkers

Agriculture—Vocational guidance
    UF   Agriculture as a profession

Agriculture—Vocational guidance for women
    RT   Agriculturists, Women

Agriculture as a profession
  USE   Agriculture—Vocational guidance

LC **Agriculturists**
    RT   Farmers
    NT   Agriculturists, Women
    UF   Agronomists

Agriculturists, Women
    BT   Agriculturists
           Women—Employment
    RT   Agriculture—Vocational guidance for women
           Farmers, Women
    UF   Women agriculturists
           Women agronomists

Agronomists
  USE   Agriculturists

Al-Anon family groups
    RT   Alcoholism and the family
           Alateen groups

Alateen groups
    RT   Al-Anon family groups
           Alcoholism and the family
           Children of alcoholic parents

Alcoholic women
    BT   Alcoholics
    UF   Women alcoholics
           Women drunkards

LC **Alcoholics**
    NT   Alcoholic women
    UF   Drunkards
           Inebriates

Alcoholism and the family
    BT   Family
    RT   Al-Anon family groups
           Alateen groups
    NT   Children of alcoholic parents
    UF   Families of alcoholics
           Family, Alcoholism and the
           The family and alcoholism

LCSH: Agricultural laborers

LCSH: Alcohol and women. *In addition, it is recommended that all other LCSH Alcohol and . . . forms that relate to classes of people be restructured on this pattern.*

LC **Alienation (Social psychology)**
     NT   Absenteeism (Labor)
     UF   Alienation, Social
              Estrangement (Social psychology)
              Social alienation

Alienation, Social
    USE   Alienation (Social psychology)

LC **Alimony**
     BT   Divorce
              Support (Domestic relations)
     RT   Child support (Law)

Alternative lifestyles
     RT   Sexual freedom
     NT   Communal lifestyles
              Family alternatives
              Marriage alternatives
              Seniors—Alternative lifestyles
     UF   Lifestyles, Alternative

LC **Amazons**
     BT   Women in folklore and mythology

American literature—Feminist authors
    USE   Feminist literature—American authors

American literature—History and criticism—Feminist perspective
     BT   Literature—History and criticism—Feminist perspective
     RT   Sex role in literature (American)

American literature, Sex role in
    USE   Sex role in literature (American)

American poetry—Feminist authors
    USE   Feminist poetry—American authors

Anarcha-feminism
    USE   Feminism, Anarchist

LC **Anarchism and anarchists**
     NT   Feminism, Anarchist
     UF   Anarchy

Anarchist feminism
    USE   Feminism, Anarchist

Anarchy
    USE   Anarchism and anarchists

Anatomy, Female (Human)
    USE   Human anatomy—Female

Anatomy, Human
    USE   Human anatomy

Anatomy, Male (Human)
    USE   Human anatomy—Male

Androgyny
     BT   Sex role
     RT   Manhood (Psychology)
              Sex differences
              Womanhood (Psychology)
     UF   Unisexuality

Androgyny in language
     BT   Sociolinguistics
     RT   Sexism and language
     UF   Language, Androgyny in

Androphobia
    USE   Hatred of men

Annulment, Marriage
    USE   Marriage—Annulment

Another Mother for Peace
    BT   Vietnamese conflict, 1961–1975—Protest movements, Women's

Anthropology, Biblical
  USE   Man and woman (Christian theology)
           Man and woman (Jewish theology)

Anthropology, Doctrinal
  USE   Man and woman (Theology)

Anthropology, Theological
  USE   Man and woman (Theology)

Anti-feminists
  USE   Feminism, Opposition to

Anti-rape movements
    BT   Women's projects and services
    RT   Rape—Law and legislation, Discriminatory
           Rape crisis centers
    NT   Self defense for women
    UF   Rape—Law reform movement
           Rape—Self-help and law reform movement

Anti-slavery movements (United States)
  USE   Slavery in the United States—Anti-slavery movements

Anti-slavery movements and feminism (United States)
  USE   Feminism and the anti-slavery movements (United States)

Anti-war protest movements (1961–1975)
  USE   Vietnamese conflict, 1961–1975—Protest movements

Anti-woman-battering movements
    BT   Women's projects and services
    RT   Woman battering—Law and legislation
           Women's shelters
    UF   Woman battering—Law reform movement
           Woman battering—Self-help and law reform movement

Apparel, Women's
  USE   Women's clothing

Artificial impregnation, Human
  USE   Artificial insemination, Human

LC **Artificial insemination, Human**
    RT   Sperm banks
           Sterilization of men (Birth control)
    UF   Artificial impregnation, Human
           Human artificial impregnation
           Human artificial insemination
           Insemination, Artificial (Human)

LC **Artificial insemination, Human—Law and legislation**
    BT   Sex and law

Aspirations, Student
  USE   Student aspirations

Assault, Criminal (Against women)
  USE   Rape
           Woman battering

LC **Assertiveness (Psychology)**
    BT   Psychology
    RT   Aggressiveness (Psychology)

Assertiveness (Psychology) in women
    BT   Sex role socialization of women
           Women—Psychology
    RT   Assertiveness training for women
    UF   Women—Assertiveness

Assertiveness training for women
    RT   Assertiveness (Psychology) in women

Athletics coaches
   NT   Athletics coaches, Women
   UF   Coaches, Athletics

Athletics coaches, Women
   BT   Athletics coaches
   UF   Women athletics coaches
           Women coaches (Athletics)

Athletics coaches, Women—Status
   BT   Sex discrimination in employment
   UF   Status of athletics coaches (Women)
   UF   Status of women athletics coaches

LC **Attitudes (Psychology)**
   NT   Job satisfaction
           Medical personnel—Attitudes
           Police—Attitudes
           Teachers—Attitudes
           Women—Employment—Attitudes of employers
           Women—Employment—Attitudes of men
           Women—Employment—Self attitude

Aunts and uncles
   UF   Uncles

LC **Authors**

Authors, Boy
   BT   Authors, Child
           Authors, Men
   UF   Boy authors

Authors, Child
   NT   Authors, Boy
           Authors, Girl
   UF   Child authors

Authors, Girl
   BT   Authors, Child
           Authors, Women
   UF   Girl authors

Authors, Homosexual
Here are entered works on authors who are homosexuals. Works on the representation of homosexuals in literature are entered under HOMOSEXUALS IN LITERATURE.
   NT   Authors, Homosexual men
           Authors, Lesbian
   UF   Gay authors
           Homosexual authors

Authors, Homosexual men
   BT   Authors, Homosexual; cf. note under AUTHORS, HOMOSEXUAL
           Authors, Men
   UF   Homosexual men authors

Authors, Lesbian
   BT   Authors, Homosexual; cf. note under AUTHORS, HOMOSEXUAL
           Authors, Women
   UF   Lesbian authors

Authors, Men
   NT   Authors, Boy
           Authors, Teen age men
           Authors, Homosexual men
   UF   Men authors

Authors, Nun
   BT   Authors, Women
   UF   Nun authors
           Nuns as authors

LCSH: Coaches (Athletics)

LCSH: Aunts, Maiden aunts. *These LCSH headings are assigned primarily to juvenile works, often with the subdivision* Fiction. *LCSH has no heading for* Uncles *although there is justification for such a heading in the literature.*

LCSH: Children as authors

LCSH: Authors

LCSH: Nuns as authors

Authors, Teen age
    NT   Authors, Teen age men
            Authors, Teen age women
    UF   Teen age authors

Authors, Teen age men   *LCSH:* Young men as authors
    BT   Authors, Men
            Authors, Teen age
    UF   Teen age men authors

Authors, Teen age women
    BT   Authors, Teen age
            Authors, Women
    UF   Teen age women authors

Authors, Women   *LCSH:* Women authors
    NT   Authors, Girl
            Authors, Lesbian
            Authors, Nun
            Authors, Teen age women
    UF   Women authors

Autoeroticism
    USE   Masturbation

LC **Automation—Social aspects**
    BT   Technology—Social aspects
    NT   Automation and women's employment

Automation and women's employment
Here are entered works on the effect of automation on routine work tasks
traditionally performed by women.
    BT   Automation—Social aspects
            Technology and women's employment

Bachelors
    USE   Single men

Bankers, Women
    RT   Banks and bankers, Women's
    UF   Women bankers

Banking
    USE   Banks and banking

Banks, Sperm
    USE   Sperm banks

LC **Banks and banking**
    RT   Credit unions
    NT   Banks and banking, Women's
    UF   Banking

Banks and banking, Cooperative
    USE   Credit unions

Banks and banking, Women's
    BT   Women's projects and services
    RT   Bankers, Women
            Feminist credit unions
    UF   Women's banks

Bat mitzvah
    USE   Bas mitzvah

Bas mitzvah
    BT   Jewish teen age women—Religious life
    UF   Bat mitzvah

Battered children
    USE   Child battering

Battered wives
    USE   Wife battering

Battered women
    USE   Woman battering

Belly dancing
  RT   Body awareness training for women

Bible—Anthropology
  USE   Man and woman (Christian theology)
       Man and woman (Jewish theology)

Bible—Stories
  USE   Bible stories

LC **Bible stories**
Here are entered accounts of Biblical events designed primarily for children.
  NT   Bible stories, Women in
  UF   Bible—Stories

Bible stories, Women in
  cf.   note under WOMEN IN THE BIBLE
  BT   Women in children's literature
  RT   Women in the Bible
  UF   Women in Bible stories

Biblical anthropology
  USE   Man and woman (Christian theology)
       Man and woman (Jewish theology)

Birth
  USE   Childbirth

LC **Birth control**
  BT   Family planning
  RT   Birth control clinics
  NT   Abortion
       Contraceptives
       Rhythm method (Birth control)
       Sterilization (Birth control)
  UF   Conception—Prevention
       Contraception

Birth control—Effectiveness

Birth control—Law and legislation
  BT   Sex and law

Birth control—Mental and physiological effects
  UF   Birth control—Physiological effects
       Birth control—Psychological aspects

Birth control—Physiological effects
  USE   Birth control—Mental and physiological effects

Birth control—Psychological aspects
  USE   Birth control—Mental and physiological effects

Birth control clinics
  BT   Women's projects and services
  RT   Birth control
  NT   Vasectomy clinics and referral services

Birth control devices
  USE   Contraceptives

Birth control pills
  USE   Oral contraceptives

LC **Bisexuality**
  BT   Sexuality

Black Americans
  USE   African-Americans; and AFRICAN-AMERICAN WOMEN, AFRICAN-
       AMERICAN GIRLS, etc.

Blacks—United States
  USE   African-Americans; and AFRICAN-AMERICAN WOMEN, AFRICAN-
       AMERICAN GIRLS, etc.

Body awareness training for women
  BT   Women—Health

LCSH: Belly dance

In LCSH both Psychological aspects *and* Physiological effects *are used as standard subdivisions; that is, they may be used to subdivide any appropriate heading. The subdivision* Mental and physiological effects *is used in LCSH to subdivide headings for topics in which the mental and physical effects are closely interrelated. Since the mental and physiological effects of birth control are often interrelated, the use of the nonstandard subdivision,* Mental and physiological effects, *is recommended.*

BT   Women—Psychology
RT   Belly dancing

Book trade
USE   Publishers and publishing

Books for children
USE   Children's literature

Boy authors
USE   Authors, Boy

Boys
Here are entered works on men from the time of birth through age 12.
BT   Men
Parent and child

Boys—Crime
USE   Juvenile delinquents (Male)

Boys—Sex role socialization
USE   Sex role socialization of children

Boys, Delinquent
USE   Juvenile delinquents (Male)

Boys' detention homes
USE   Juvenile detention homes (Male)

Boys' Reformatories
USE   Reformatories (Male)

Breast cancer
BT   Women—Diseases
RT   Breast examination

Breast cancer—Surgery
RT   Breast protheses
Mastectomy counseling and therapy
UF   Lumpectomy
Mastectomy
Radical mastectomy

Breast examination
RT   Breast cancer
NT   Mammography

LC **Breast feeding**
UF   Nursing (Infant feeding)
Suckling (Infant feeding)

Breast protheses
RT   Breast cancer—Surgery

Breast radiography
USE   Mammography

LC **Business**
RT   Business personnel
UF   Business administration
Trade

LC **Business—Vocational guidance**
BT   Vocational guidance
NT   Business—Vocational guidance for men
Business—Vocational guidance for women
UF   Business as a profession

Business—Vocational guidance for men
BT   Business—Vocational guidance
RT   Businessmen

Business—Vocational guidance for women
BT   Business—Vocational guidance
RT   Businesswomen

Business, Choice of
USE   Vocational guidance

LCSH: Breast—Cancer. *There is not any real quarrel with the LCSH form; the unsubdivided form is simply more direct and reflects the way people think. (Both forms would file in the same place in a straight word for word alphabetical sequence.) LCSH does not use any of the UF references listed.*

LCSH: Breast—Examination

Business administration
USE   Business

Business as a profession
USE   Business—Vocational guidance

Business executives
USE   Executives

Business men
USE   Businessmen

LC **Business personnel**   *LCSH:* Businessmen; Women in
Here are entered works on people in business management. Works on   business
people in clerical and secretarial positions are entered under OFFICE
WORKERS.
RT   Business
NT   Businessmen
        Businesswomen
        Executives
UF   Businesspeople

Business women
USE   Businesswomen
        Executives, Women

LC **Businessmen**
BT   Business personnel
RT   Business—Vocational guidance for men
UF   Business men
        Men in business

Businesspeople
USE   Business personnal

Businesswomen
BT   Business personnel
        Women—Employment
RT   Business—Vocational guidance for women
NT   Executives, Women
UF   Business women
        Women in business

Businesswomen—Status
BT   Sex discrimination in employment
UF   Status of women in business
        Status of businesswomen

Caesarian section
USE   Cesarian section

Cantors (Jewish)   *LCSH:* Cantors, Jewish
UF   Jewish Cantors

Cantors, Women (Jewish)
UF   Jewish women cantors
        Women cantors (Jewish)

Career-family conflict, Women's
USE   Women—Education—Role conflict
        Women—Employment—Role conflict

Career education
USE   Vocational education

Careers
USE   Occupations
        Professions
        Vocational guidance

Catholic church—Volunteer women workers
USE   Church workers (Volunteer), Women—Catholic Church

Catholic Church—Women workers (Volunteer)
USE   Church workers (Volunteer), Women—Catholic Church

Catholic Church [Church of England; Lutheran Church, etc.]—Prayer books and devotions for women.
    BT   Women—Prayer books and devotions
    UF   Catholic Church [Church of England, Lutheran Church, etc.]—
             Prayer books and devotions for women—English
Catholic Church [Church of England, Lutheran Church, etc.]—Prayer books and devotions for women—English
    USE   Catholic Church [Church of England, Lutheran Church, etc.]—
               Prayer books and devotions for women
Catholic Church and women
    BT   Christianity and women
    NT   Ordination of women—Catholic Church
            Vatican Council, 2d, 1962–1965 and women
    UF   Women and the Catholic Church
Catholic nuns
    USE   Nuns, Catholic
Catholic sisters
    USE   Nuns, Catholic
LC **Cesarian section**
    BT   Obstetrics—Surgery
    UF   Caesarian section
            Childbirth—Cesarian section
Change of life in men
    USE   Climacteric
Change of life in women
    USE   Climacteric
            Menopause
Change of life pregnancy
    USE   Middle age women—Pregnancy
Change of sex
    USE   Transsexual surgery
Chicanas
    USE   Latino women—United States
            Mexican-American women
Chicano women
    USE   Latino women—United States
            Mexican-American women
Child abuse
    USE   Child battering
            Cruelty to children
Child adoption
    USE   Adoption
Child and father
    USE   Father and child
Child and mother
    USE   Mother and child
Child and parent
    USE   Parent and child
Child authors
    USE   Authors, Child
Child battering
    BT   Cruelty to children
            Household violence
    RT   Woman battering
    UF   Battered children
            Child abuse
Child-bearing
    USE   Pregnancy

LC assigns Women—Prayer books and devotions *and* [Church]—Prayer books and devotions *to denominational prayer books designed for use by women (the armed forces, men, girls, etc.). The result is two nonspecific headings.*

Child birth
 USE   Childbirth

Child care
  BT   Civil rights—Women
  RT   Absenteeism (Labor)—Women
        Child care centers
        Mothers—Employment
  UF   Day care
        Foster day care

Child care—Feminist perspective
  BT   Human resources policy—Feminist perspective

Task Force on Working Women. Exploitation from 9 to 5. (1975) "The lack of good, reasonably priced and convenient child care is a major barrier to equal rights for women" p. 169. "Child care is a complex issue, but without child care, the right of women to work will not be a reality. . . . It should be clear, however, that custodial child care is not what parents and children want. Child care should, by now, be synonymous with an educational experience" p. 185.

Child care centers
  RT   Child care
        Education, Preschool
        Nursery schools
  UF   Day care centers
        Day nurseries
        Foster day care

LCSH: Day care centers

Child care leave
  BT   Leave of absence (Employment)

Child care leave (Father)
  BT   Men—Employment
  NT   Reverse sex discrimination in child care leave
  UF   Paternity leave

Child care leave (Mother)
Here are entered works on leaves of absence from employment to care for
dependent children. Works on leaves of absence connected with the birth
of a child are entered under MATERNITY LEAVE.
  BT   Women—Employment
  RT   Maternity leave
  NT   Sex discrimination in maternity and child care leave

Child care leave (Mother), Sex discrimination in
 USE   Sex discrimination in maternity and child care leave

Child custody
  BT   Divorce
        Parent and child (Law)
  RT   Children of divorced parents
  NT   Men and child custody
        Women and child custody
  UF   Children—Custody
        Children, Custody of
        Custody of children
        Parental custody

LCSH: Custody of children

Child custody and homosexual men
 USE   Homosexual men and child custody

Child custody and lesbians
 USE   Lesbians and child custody

Child custody and men
  USE   Men and child custody

Child custody and women
  USE   Women and child custody

Child-free marriage
  BT   Family alternatives
         Family planning
         Marriage alternatives
  UF   Childless marriage
         Marriage, Child-free
         Marriage, Childless

Child-mother relationship
  USE   Mother and child

Child-nurses
  UF   Nursemaids

Child placing
  USE   Adoption

Child prostitutes
  USE   Prostitutes (Child)

Child rearing
  USE   Children—Development and guidance

Child support (Law)
  BT   Divorce
         Parent and child (Law)
         Support (Domestic relations)
  RT   Alimony

Childbirth
  BT   Obstetrics
         Pregnancy
  NT   Childbirth at home
         Natural childbirth
  UF   Birth
         Child birth
         Human birth
         Parturition

Childbirth—Cesarian section
  USE   Cesarian section

Childbirth—Labor
  NT   Natural childbirth
  UF   Labor (Childbirth)

Childbirth—Labor, Complicated
  UF   Placenta previa

Childbirth—Labor, Induced
  UF   Induced labor (Childbirth)

Childbirth—Labor, Premature
  UF   Premature labor (Childbirth)

LC **Childbirth—Psychological aspects**
  RT   Natural childbirth

Childbirth, Natural
  USE   Natural childbirth

Childbirth at home
  BT   Childbirth
  RT   Midwives
         Natural childbirth
  UF   Home childbirth

Childless marriage
  USE   Child-free marriage

Children—Custody
  USE   Child custody

LCSH uses Childbirth, Labor (Obstetrics), *and* Parturition *(the last only recently established). This abundance of terms may be well justified by their collection, but it would not make much sense in most general or women's library collections. The use of* Childbirth *as a single term is recommended; the specific headings relating to labor have been made subdivisions of* Childbirth.

Children—Development and guidance
  NT   Parenting
  UF   Child rearing
       Children—Management
       Children—Training
       Discipline of children
       Training of children

Children—Management
  USE   Children—Development and guidance

Children—Sex role socialization
  USE   Sex role socialization of children

Children—Sports
  USE   Sports for children

Children—Training
  USE   Children—Development and guidance

LC **Children, Adopted**
  RT   Adoption
  NT   Children adopted by a single parent
  UF   Adopted children

Children, Adopted—Personal name rights
  BT   Names, Personal—Law

Children, Cruelty to
  USE   Cruelty to children

Children, Custody of
  USE   Child custody

Children adopted by a single parent
  BT   Children, Adopted
       Children of single parents
  RT   Single-parent adoption
       Single-parent family

Children and divorce
  USE   Children of divorced parents

Children and parents
Here are entered works on the moral and social responsibilities of adult children toward their parents and on the relationship between adult children and their parents. Works on the responsibilities of parents toward minor children and on the relationship between parents and minor children are entered under PARENT AND CHILD.
  RT   Interpersonal relations
       Parent and child
  UF   Parents and children

LC **Children of alcoholic parents**
  BT   Alcoholism and the family
       Parent and child
  RT   Alateen groups

LC **Children of divorced parents**
  BT   Children of single parents
       Divorce
       Parent and child
  RT   Child custody
       Father-separated children
       Mother-separated children
       Single-parent family
  UF   Children and divorce
       Divorce and children

Children of homosexual parents
  BT   Parent and child
  RT   Homosexual parents
  UF   Homosexual parents, Children of

LCSH: Children—Management

Children of older parents
BT   Parent and child
RT   Parenting and middle age

Children of single parents
Here are entered works on children of unmarried parents and of parents
who are single through divorce, desertion, widowhood, single-parent
adoption, etc.
BT   Parent and child
RT   Single fathers
Single mothers
Single-parent family
NT   Children of divorced parents
Children adopted by a single parent
UF   Single parents, Children of
Unmarried parents, Children of

Children of unmarried couples
BT   Parent and child
RT   Unmarried couples
UF   Unmarried couples, Children of
Unmarried parents, Children of

Children's books
USE   Children's literature

LC **Children's films**
Here are entered individual fiction and nonfiction films produced primarily
for children. Entry is also made under the subject matter of the film.
BT   Motion pictures
UF   Films, Children's
Juvenile films
Motion pictures for children
Moving pictures for children

LC **Children's films—History and criticism**

Children's films, Nonsexist
BT   Teaching materials, Nonsexist
UF   Nonsexist children's films

LC **Children's literature**
UF   Books for children
Children's books
Juvenile literature

Children's literature, Men in
USE   Men in children's literature

Children's literature, Nonsexist
BT   Sex role in children's literature
Teaching materials, Nonsexist
RT   Sexism in children's literature
UF   Nonsexist children's literature

Children's literature, Sex role in
USE   Sex role in children's literature

Children's literature, Sexism in
USE   Sexism in children's literature

Children's literature, Women in
USE·   Women in children's literature

Children's prisons
USE   Juvenile detention homes

Choice of profession
USE   Vocational guidance

Christian feminism
USE   Feminism, Christian

Christian feminists
USE   Feminism, Christian

LCSH assigns the heading Children's
films *to "individual fiction films which
are produced primarily for children."
Works on fiction films are assigned*
Children's films—History and criticism;
*works on both fiction and nonfiction
films are assigned* Moving pictures for
children. *One gathers from these instructions that the heading* Children's
films *is not assigned to nonfiction films.
It is recommended that* Children's films
*be assigned to all films produced for
children. It is further recommended
that the fine distinction between the
headings for works on children's fiction
and nonfiction films be abandoned. The
distinction is too fine; it splits the material and can only prove confusing to a
user. All works on films for children
should be entered under* Children's
films—History and criticism.

Christian life
  USE   Religious life (Christianity)

Christian men—Biography
  BT   Christians—Biography

Christian nuns
  USE   Nuns, Christian

Christian religious tradition and feminism
  USE   Judaeo-Christian religious tradition—Feminist perspective

Christian sisters
  USE   Nuns, Christian

Christian women
  BT   Women
  RT   Christianity and women
  UF   Women, Christian

Christian women—Biography
  BT   Christians—Biography

Christian women—Congresses

Christianity and feminism
  USE   Feminism, Christian
        Judaeo-Christian religious tradition—Feminist perspective

Christianity and sex
  USE   Sex and Christianity

Christianity and women
Here are entered works on the status of women in the Christian tradition.
For works on the theological position of women in Christianity see WOMEN
(CHRISTIAN THEOLOGY). For works on the day-to-day religious practice of
Christian women see RELIGIOUS LIFE (CHRISTIANITY)—WOMEN.
  BT   Religion and women
  RT   Christian women
        Judaeo-Christian religious tradition—Feminist perspective
        Religious life (Christianity)—Women
        Woman (Christian theology)
  NT   CATHOLIC CHURCH AND WOMEN; CHURCH OF ENGLAND AND WOMEN
        and similar headings.
  UF   Women and Christianity
        Women in Christianity

Christians—Biography
  NT   Christian men—Biography
        Christian women—Biography

Church of England and women
  BT   Christianity and women
  NT   Ordination of women—Church of England
  UF   Women and the Church of England

Church workers (Volunteer)
  BT   Volunteer work and workers
  NT   Church workers (Volunteer), Women
  UF   Volunteer church workers

Church workers (Volunteer), Women
  BT   Church workers (Volunteer)
  UF   Women church workers (Volunteer)
        Women in church work (Volunteer)

Church workers (Volunteer), Women—Catholic Church [Church of England, Lutheran Church, etc.]
  UF   Catholic Church—Volunteer women workers
        Catholic Church—Women workers (Volunteer)

LC **Civil rights**
  NT   Affirmative action
  NT   Women—Civil rights
  UF   Human rights
        Rights, Civil

LCSH practice is to assign two headings, neither of them specific, to works on Christian women; e.g., a collected biography is assigned the headings Women—Biography and Christian biography; the proceedings of a conference on women's role in the ecumenical movement is assigned the headings Women—Congresses and Christian union—Congresses.

LCSH: Christian biography. This change is recommended both because the term is inaccurate (the biography is not Christian) and because the dash subdivision is used under all other classes of persons; e.g. Jews—Biography, Children—Biography, etc.

LCSH: Women in church work. "Volunteer" was added to limit the scope of the heading. The LCSH heading is assigned to works on both volunteer and professional (e.g., nuns, ministers, deacons) church workers.

Civil service, Sex discrimination in
   USE   Sex discrimination in government employment

Civilians' work in war time
   USE   War—Civilians' work

Cleaning women
   USE   Household workers, Women

Clergywomen (Christianity)
   RT   Rabbis, Women
   NT   Ordination of women (Christianity)
   UF   Ministers, Women
            Priests, Women
            Women clergy
            Women ministers
            Women priests

> *LCSH:* Clergy, Clergymen, Women ministers

Clerical employees
   USE   Clerks

LC **Clerks**
   BT   Office workers
   RT   Clerks (Retail trade)
   UF   Clerical employees
            Employees, Clerical

Clerks, Women
   UF   Women clerks

LC **Clerks (Retail trade)**
   BT   White collar workers
   RT   Clerks
            Sales personnel
   UF   Clerks (Sales personnel)
            Retail clerks
            Salesclerks
            Stores, Retail—Employees

Clerks (Retail trade), Women
   UF   Women clerks

Clerks (Sales personnel)
   USE   Clerks (Retail trade)

LC **Climacteric**
   NT   Menopause
   UF   Change of life in men
            Change of life in women

Clincs, Women's
   USE   Women's health centers and clinics

Clitoral orgasm
   USE   Orgasm, Clitoral

Clothing, Women's
   USE   Women's clothing

Clothing and dress
Here are entered general works dealing with clothes as a covering for the body and works on the art of dress.
   NT   Men's clothing
            Women's clothing

> *LCSH uses this heading for works on clothing and dress in general and for works on women's clothing. (Just the opposite of what usually happens in the list where terms are used for general works and for works on men.)* Women's clothing *has been established in this list. The references to particular items of women's clothing (e.g.* Bloomer costume *(!) and* Blouses*) which are listed under* Clothing and dress *should be listed under* Women's clothing.

Coaches, Athletics
   USE   Athletics coaches

LC **Coeducation**
   BT   Education

Coeducation—Feminist perspective

Cohabitation
   USE   Unmarried couples

Coil (Birth control device)
   USE   Intrauterine contraceptives

College graduate men
- BT   College graduates
- UF   Men college graduates

College graduate men—Employment
- BT   Men—Employment
- UF   Employment—Men college graduates

College graduate women
- BT   College graduates
- UF   Women college graduates

College graduate women—Employment
- BT   Women—Employment
- UF   Employment—Women college graduates

LC **College graduates**
- NT   College graduate men
         College graduate women
- UF   University graduates

Colleges
- USE   Universities and colleges

Comarital relations
- USE   Extramarital relations

Comic books, strips, etc.
- NT   Comic books, strips, etc., Women's
- UF   Comic strips
         Comics
         Funnies

Comic books, strips, etc., Women's
- BT   Comic books, strips, etc.
         Mass media, Women's
         Periodicals, Women's
         Women's presses
- UF   Comic books, Women's
         Women's comic books, strips, etc.
         Women's comic strips
         Women's comix

Comic books, Women's
- USE   Comic books, strips, etc., Women's

Comic strips
- USE   Comic books, strips, etc.

Comics
- USE   Comic books, strips, etc.

Commercial employees
- USE   Office workers

LC **Common law marriage**
- BT   Marriage alternatives
         Unmarried couples
- UF   Marriage, Common law

Communal family
Here are entered works on people living in formally organized communes.
Works on families, or other groups of people, who have loosely organized
themselves, in the manner of an extended family, to provide mutual
support in time of need are entered under COMMUNALLY ORGANIZED GROUPS.
- BT   Communal lifestyles
- RT   Communally organized groups
- UF   Family, Communal
         Family networks
         Networks of families

Communal lifestyles
- BT   Alternative lifestyles
         Family alternatives
- NT   Communal family

NT   Communally organized groups
UF   Lifestyles, Communal

Communally organized groups
cf.   note under COMMUNAL FAMILY.
BT   Communal lifestyles
RT   Communal family
UF   Family, Communal
       Family networks
       Networks of families

Compensation
USE   Pensions
       Wages

Conception—Prevention
USE   Birth control

LC **Condoms**
BT   Contraceptives
UF   Prophylactic (Birth control device)
       "Rubbers" (Birth control device)

Congressmen and -women
USE   Legislators—United States

Congresswomen (House)
BT   Legislators, Women—United States

Congresswomen (Senate)
USE   Senators (United States), Women

Consciousness-raising (Technique)
RT   Consciousness-raising groups
       Women's movement (1960–   )—Organizing tactics

Consciousness-raising groups
RT   Consciousness-raising (Technique)
NT   Consciousness-raising groups, Men's
       Consciousness-raising groups, Women's

Consciousness-raising groups, Men's
BT   Consciousness-raising groups
RT   Men's liberation
UF   Men's consciousness-raising groups

Consciousness-raising groups, Women's
BT   Consciousness-raising groups
UF   Women's consciousness-raising groups

Consensual adultery
USE   Extramarital relations

LC **Consumer credit**
NT   Sex discrimination in consumer credit
UF   Credit, Consumer

Consumer credit, Sex discrimination in
USE   Sex discrimination in consumer credit

Continuing education
USE   Adult education

Contraception
USE   Birth control

LC **Contraceptives**
BT   Birth control
NT   Condoms
       Diaphragm (Birth control device)
       Intrauterine contraceptives
       Oral contraceptives
UF   Birth control devices

Contraceptives—Effectiveness

Contraceptives—Mental and Physiological effects
UF   Contraceptives—Physiological effects
       Contraceptives—Psychological aspects

Contraceptives—Physiological effects
USE   Contraceptives—Mental and physiological effects

Contraceptives—Psychological aspects
USE   Contraceptives—Mental and physiological effects

Contraceptives—Research

Contraceptives, Oral
USE   Oral contraceptives

Contract cohabitation
USE   Contractual marriage

Contractual marriage
BT   Marriage alternatives
      Unmarried couples
RT   Marriage contracts, Extralegal; cf. note under MARRIAGE
      CONTRACTS, EXTRALEGAL
UF   Contract cohabitation
      Marriage, Contractual

Convicts
USE   Prisoners

Cooperative banks
USE   Credit unions

Core curriculum
USE   Education—Curricula

Corporation executives
USE   Executives

LC **Counseling**
NT   Counseling, Nonsexist
      Counseling for men
      Counseling for women
      Divorce and separation counseling
      Feminist counseling and therapy
      Marriage counseling
      Sex counseling and therapy
      Sexism in counseling
      Vocational guidance

Counseling, Nonsexist
BT   Counseling
RT   Counseling for men
      Counseling for women
      Feminist counseling and therapy
      Sexism in counseling
UF   Nonsexist counseling

Counseling, Nonsexist—Study and teaching

Counseling for girls
BT   Counseling for women
NT   Vocational guidance for girls
UF   Girls—Counseling
      Girls, Counseling for

Counseling for men
BT   Counseling
RT   Counseling, Nonsexist
      Sexism in counseling
NT   Vasectomy counseling
UF   Men—Counseling
      Men, Counseling for

Counseling for middle age women
BT   Counseling for women
NT   Pregnancy counseling for middle age women
      Vocational guidance for women reentering employment
UF   Middle age women—Counseling
      Middle age women, Counseling for

Counseling for senior women
   BT   Counseling for women
   NT   Vocational guidance for women reentering employment
   UF   Senior women—Counseling
           Senior women, Counseling for

Counseling for teen age women
   BT   Counseling for women
   NT   Pregnancy counseling for teen age women
           Teen age women's projects and services
           Vocational guidance for teen age women
   UF   Teen age women—Counseling
           Teen age women, Counseling for

Counseling for women
Here are entered works on women as the recipients of counseling. Works on career opportunities for women in counseling are entered under COUNSELING—VOCATIONAL GUIDANCE FOR WOMEN.

cf. LCSH Counseling for clergy *for LCSH subject heading pattern authority.*

   BT   Counseling
           Women's projects and services
   RT   Counseling, Nonsexist
           Feminist counseling and therapy
           Sexism in counseling
   NT   Abortion counseling
           Academic counseling for women
           Counseling for girls
           Counseling for middle age women
           Counseling for senior women
           Counseling for teen age women
           Mastectomy counseling and therapy
           Miscarriage counseling
           Pregnancy counseling
           Vocational guidance for women
   UF   Women—Counseling
           Women, Counseling for

Counseling, Feminist
  USE   Feminist counseling and therapy

Counseling, Marital
  USE   Marriage counseling

Counseling, Sexism in
  USE   Counseling, Nonsexist
           Sexism in counseling

Counselors, Women
   BT   Professional women
   UF   Women counselors

Counselors, Women—Status
   BT   Professional women—Status
           Sex discrimination in employment
   UF   Status of women counselors
           Status of counselors (Women)

Couples, Homosexual
  USE   Homosexual couples

Couples, Lesbian
  USE   Lesbian couples

Couples, Unmarried
  USE   Unmarried couples

Courses of study
  USE   Education—Curricula

The craft, Feminism and
  USE   Feminist wicci and wicceans

Credit, Consumer
  USE   Consumer credit

Credit cooperatives
USE   Credit unions

Credit Unions
RT   Banks and banking
NT   Feminist credit unions
UF   Banks and banking, Cooperative
Cooperative banks
Credit cooperatives
People's banks

LCSH: Banks and banking, Cooperative. *There is not a real objection to the LCSH form;* Credit unions *is simply more current.*

Credit unions, Feminist
USE   Feminist credit unions

LC **Crime and criminals (Indirect)**
Works on criminal members of ethnic, racial, religious, or sexual groups, and works on criminals of a specific nationality operating outside of their country of national origin are entered also under CRIMINALS, [ETHNIC, RACIAL, NATIONAL, ETC. MODIFIER]; e.g. CRIMINALS, AFRICAN-AMERICAN, CRIMINALS, CATHOLIC, CRIMINALS, IRISH, CRIMINALS, ITALIAN-AMERICAN, CRIMINALS, JEWISH, CRIMINALS, WOMEN
RT   Prisons
Prisoners
NT   CRIMINALS, MEN; CRIMINALS, WOMEN and similar headings
Juvenile delinquency

LCSH presently singles out four classes of persons (Blacks, Catholics, Jews, and women) who, if they are criminals, transcend their nationality. All other criminals are entered under Crime and criminals—Geographic subdivision. *In order to increase and unbias access, it is recommended that a work, for instance, on Irish criminals in the U.S. be entered under both* Crime and criminals—United States *and* Criminals, Irish—United States *(or, if the work is on Irish-American criminals: under* Criminals—Irish-American*). A work on women criminals in Great Britain would be entered under both* Crime and criminals—Great Britain *and* Criminals, Women—Great Britain. *The present references from LCSH* Crime and criminals *to named criminal groups that are associated with specific ethnic, national, etc. groups should be made references to the specific ethnic, national, etc. group; e.g.* Criminals, Irish—United States *should have a NT reference to* Molly Maguires. Mafia, *on the other hand, should remain as a reference under* Crime and criminals *since one can hardly say that all Mafia business is conducted by Italians or Italian-Americans.*

Crimes against the person
USE   Offenses against the person

Criminal assault against women
USE   Rape
Woman battering

Criminals, Men (Indirect)
BT   Crime and criminals
Men
RT   Prisoners, Men
Prisons for men
NT   Juvenile delinquents (Male)
UF   Men—Crime
Men criminals
Men offenders
Offenders, Men

Criminals, Women (Indirect)
BT   Crime and criminals
Women
RT   Prisoners, Women
Prisons for women
NT   Juvenile delinquents (Female)
UF   Offenders, Women
Women—Crime
Women criminals
Women offenders

LCSH: Female offenders; *with a see reference from* Delinquent women *(the former LCSH heading for works on the topic).*

Crisis housing, Women's
USE   Women's shelters

Cross-dressing
USE   Transvestism

LC **Cruelty to children**
BT   Offenses against the person
NT   Child battering
UF   Child abuse
Children, cruelty to

Curricula (Courses of study)
USE   Education—Curricula

Custody of children
USE   Child custody

Cycles, Menstrual
USE   Menstruation

Daughters and fathers
USE   Fathers and daughters

Daughters and mothers
USE   Mothers and daughters

Day care
USE   Child care

Day nurseries
USE   Child care centers

Day workers (Domestic)
USE   Household workers

Defense work in war-time, Civilian
USE   War—Civilians' work

Delinquency, Juvenile
USE   Juvenile delinquency
       Juvenile delinquents

LC **Dental assistants**
    BT   Paraprofessions and paraprofessionals
    NT   Dental assistants, Women

Dental assistants, Women
    BT   Dental assistants
    UF   Women dental assistants

Deprivation, Maternal
USE   Mother-separated children

Deprivation, Parental
USE   Parent-separated children

Deprivation, Paternal
USE   Father-separated children

LC **Desertion and nonsupport**
    BT   Parent and child (Law)
    RT   Married men—Legal status, laws, etc.
          Runaway wives, husbands, etc.
          Support (Domestic relations)
    UF   Abandonment of family
          Nonsupport (Domestic relations)

Detention homes, Juvenile
USE   Juvenile detention homes

Diaphragm (Birth control device)
    BT   Contraceptives
    UF   Vaginal diaphragms

Discipleship (Christianity)
USE   Religious life (Christianity)

Discipline of children
USE   Children—Development and guidance

LC **Discrimination**
    NT   Age discrimination in employment
          Homophobia
          Reverse sex discrimination
          Sex discrimination
          headings beginning with the word DISCRIMINATION

Discrimination, Sex
USE   Reverse sex discrimination
       Sex discrimination

Discrimination against Gays
USE   Homophobia

LCSH: Diaphragms, Vaginal. *The LCSH heading gives the impression that the diaphragm is organic. The heading recommended is modeled after the LCSH* Diaphragms (Mechanical devices).

Discrimination against homosexuals
  USE   Homophobia

Discrimination against men
  USE   Reverse sex discrimination

Discrimination against women
  USE   Sex discrimination

LC **Discrimination in education**
  BT   Education
  NT   Equal educational opportunity
        Sex discrimination in education
  UF   Education, Discrimination in

LC **Discrimination in employment**
  RT   Age discrimination in employment
        Minorities—Employment
  NT   Equal pay for equal work
        Sex discrimination in employment
        Sex-typing of occupations
  UF   Employment discrimination
        Fair employment practice
        Job discrimination

Discrimination in employment—Law and legislation
  BT   Labor laws and legislation
  RT   Affirmation action

LC **Discrimination in housing**
  NT   Sex discrimination in housing
  UF   Fair housing
        Housing, Discrimination in
        Open housing
        Segregation in housing

Discrimination in labor laws and legislation
  USE   Labor laws and legislation, Discriminatory

Discrimination in law and legislation, Sex
  USE   Women—Legal status, laws, etc.—
        Discriminatory legislation

LC **Discrimination in public accommodations**
  NT   Sex discrimination in public accommodations
  UF   Public accommodations, Discrimination in
        Segregation in public accommodations

Displaced housewives
  USE   Women—Employment reentry

LC **Divorce**
  BT   Marriage
  RT   Divorced people
        Husband and wife
        Marriage—Annulment
        Separation (Law)
  NT   Alimony
        Child custody
        Child support (Law)
        Children of divorced parents
        Divorce, No-fault
        Divorce and separation counseling

Divorce—Legal self-help clinics
  BT   Women's legal self-help clinics
  RT   Divorce and separation counseling
        Separation (Law)

Divorce, No-fault
  BT   Divorce
  UF   No-fault divorce

Divorce and children
  USE   Children of divorced parents

Divorce and separation counseling
    BT   Counseling
            Divorce
    RT   Divorce—Legal self-help clinics
            Marriage—Annulment
            Marriage counseling
            Separation (Law)
    UF   Divorce counseling
            Separation and divorce counseling

Divorce counseling
    USE   Divorce and separation counseling

Divorced men
    BT   Divorced people
            Single men
    RT   Single fathers
            Single parent family (Father)
    UF   Men, Divorced

Divorced people
    RT   Single parent family
    NT   Divorced men
            Divorced women
            Remarriage

Divorced people—Personal name rights
    BT   Names, Personal—Law

Divorced women
    BT   Divorced people
            Single women
    RT   Single mothers
            Single parent family (Mother)
    UF   Divorcees
            Women, Divorced

Divorced women—Legal status, laws, etc.
    RT   Married women—Legal status, laws, etc.

Divorcees
    USE   Divorced women

Doctrinal anthropology
    USE   Man and woman (Theology)

Domestic workers
    USE   Household workers

Domestics
    USE   Household workers

"Double standard"
    USE   Sexism in interpersonal relations

Drop-in centers, Women's
    USE   Women's centers and networks

Drunkards
    USE   Alcoholics

E.R.A.
    USE   Equal rights amendment (Proposed)

Early marriage
    USE   Teen age marriage

Economic planning
    USE   Economic policy

LC **Economic policy**
    NT   Human resources policy
            Labor supply
            Women's movement (1960–   ) and economic policy
    UF   Economic planning
            National planning
            Planning, Economic

LCSH: Divorcees; *since the LCSH heading is undeniably feminine, its use for works on both divorced men and divorced women serves no one.*

Economic policy (cont.)
    UF   Planning, National
            Planning, State
            Public policy
            State planning
            World economics

Economic policy—Feminist perspective
Here are entered feminist works on the conscious or unconscious
oppression of women by established economic policy.
    RT   Sex discrimination—Economic aspects
    NT   Human resources policy—Feminist perspective
            subdivision ECONOMIC POLICY—FEMINIST PERSPECTIVE under names
                of countries, cities, etc.
    UF   Feminism and economic policy
            Feminist economic policy

Economically disadvantaged
    USE   The poor

LC **Education**
    NT   Adult education
            Coeducation
            Discrimination in education
            Higher education
    NT   Men—Education
            Nursery schools
            Physical education
            Preschool education
            Primary education
            Secondary education
            Vocational education
            Women—Education
    UF   Instruction
            Pedagogy

LC **Education—Curricula**
    NT   HIGHER EDUCATION—CURRICULA; PRIMARY EDUCATION—CURRICULA
            and the subdivision CURRICULA under similar headings for
                specific types of education
    UF   Core curriculum
            Courses of study
            Curricula (Courses of study)
            Schools—Curricula
            Study, Courses of

Education—Curricula, Nonsexist
    RT   Men—Education
            Sexism in curricula
            Women—Education
    NT   Teaching materials, Nonsexist
    UF   Education—Nonsexist curricula

Education—Girls
    USE   Girls—Education

Education—Nonsexist curricula
    USE   Education—Curricula, Nonsexist

Education—Sexism in curricula
    USE   Sexism in curricula

Education—Teen age women
    USE   Teen age women—Education

Education—Women
    USE   Women—Education

Education, Continuing
    USE   Adult education

Education, Discrimination in
    USE   Discrimination in education

Education, Higher
  USE   Higher education

Education, Physical
  USE   Physical education

Education, Preschool
  USE   Preschool education

Education, Primary
  USE   Primary education

Education, Secondary
  USE   Secondary education

Education, Sex discrimination in
  USE   Sex discrimination in education

Education, Vocational
  USE   Vocational education

Education and income
  BT   Income
  UF   Income and education

Education and income—Women
  BT   Women—Education
  RT   Sex discrimination in employment

Education of adults
  USE   Adult education

Educational aspirations
  USE   Student aspirations

Educational equalization
  USE   Equal educational opportunity

Educational measurements
  USE   Educational tests and measurements

Educational media
  USE   Teaching materials

Educational opportunity, Equal
  USE   Equal educational opportunity

LC **Educational tests and measurements**
  NT   Sexism in educational tests and measurements
  UF   Educational measurements
        Tests and measurements in education

Elderly persons
  USE   Seniors

Elderly workers
  USE   Seniors—Employment
        Seniors and employment

Emancipation of women
  USE   Women—Civil rights

Emergency housing, Women's
  USE   Women's shelters

Employee absenteeism
  USE   Absenteeism (Labor)

Employees, Clerical
  USE   Clerks

LC **Employees, Training of**
  Here are entered works on the training of employees on the job. Works on retraining persons with obsolete vocational skills are entered under OCCUPATIONAL RETRAINING. Works on vocational instruction within the standard educational system are entered under VOCATIONAL EDUCATION. Works on the vocationally oriented process of endowing people with a skill after either completion or termination of their formal education are entered under OCCUPATIONAL TRAINING.
  RT   Occupational retraining
        Occupational training

Employees, Training of (cont.)
  UF   In-service training
        On the job training
        Training of employees
        Training within industry

Employees, Training of—Feminist perspective
  BT   Human resources policy—Feminist perspective
  RT   Employees (Women), Training of
  UF   Feminism and employee training
        Feminism and on the job training
        Feminism and training of employees

Employees (Men), Training of
  BT   Men—Employment
  UF   Men—Training on the job
        Men—On the job training
        Men—In-service training

Employees (Women), Training of
  BT   Women—Employment
  RT   Employees, Training of—Feminist perspective
  UF   Women—In-service training
        Women—On the job training
        Women—Training on the job

Employers' attitudes towards women workers
  USE   Women—Employment—Attitudes of employers

Employment—College graduates
  USE   College graduates—Employment

Employment—Married women
  USE   Married women—Employment

Employment—Men
  USE   Men—Employment

Employment—Men college graduates
  USE   College graduate men—Employment

Employment—Wives
  USE   Married women—Employment

Employment—Women
  USE   Women—Employment

Employment—Women, Married
  USE   Married women—Employment

Employment—Women college graduates
  USE   College graduate women—Employment

Employment, Age discrimination in
  USE   Age discrimination in employment

Employment, Part-time
  USE   Job-sharing
         Part-time employment

LC **Employment agencies**
  RT   Affirmative action organizations, centers, etc.
        Job hunting
  UF   Agencies, Employment
        Employment offices
        Job placement services

Employment and age
  USE   Age and employment

Employment and homosexuality
  USE   Homosexuality and employment

Employment and middle age
  USE   Middle age and employment

Employment and seniors
  USE   Seniors and employment

Employment and teen age
USE   Teen age and employment

Employment and youth
USE   Teen age and employment

Employment discrimination
USE   Discrimination in employment

LC **Employment interviewing**
RT   Job hunting
UF   Job interviewing

Employment interviewing, Nonsexist
BT   Women—Employment
RT   Sexism in employment interviewing
        Job hunting for women
UF   Nonsexist employment interviewing

Employment interviewing, Sexism in
USE   Sexism in employment interviewing

Employment offices
USE   Employment agencies

Enculturation
USE   Socialization

English language, Sexism in
USE   Sexism in language (English)

English literature—History and criticism—Feminist perspective
BT   Literature—History and criticism—Feminist perspective
RT   Sex role in literature (English)

English literature, Sex role in
USE   Sex role in literature (English)

Equal educational opportunity
BT   Discrimination in education
NT   Equal educational opportunity and women's status
UF   Educational equalization
        Educational opportunity, Equal

LCSH: Educational equalization

Equal educational opportunity and women's status
Here are entered works on social attitudes towards education for women and on the impact the absence of even minimal educational opportunities for women has on their potential place in society.
BT   Equal educational opportunity
        Human resources policy—Feminist perspective
        Women—Education
        Women—Social conditions

There have been many studies conducted, mainly by the United Nations, on the problem of women's full participation in society due to social attitudes towards education for women that discourage, or actually prohibit, the education of women.

LC **Equal pay for equal work**
BT   Discrimination in employment
        Wages

Equal pay for equal work—Women workers
BT   Sex discrimination in employment
RT   Sex discrimination in wages

Equal rights amendment (Proposed)
BT   Women—Civil rights—United States
        Women—Legal status, laws, etc.—United States
UF   E.R.A.
        ERA
        United States. Constitution. Equal rights amendment (Proposed)

Equal Rights Amendment (Proposed) and state legislation
Here are entered works on the effect of the passage of the Equal Rights Amendment to the United States Constitution on present state legislation regarding women.
UF   State legislation and the Equal Rights Amendment (Proposed)

ERA
USE   Equal rights amendment (Proposed)

Estrangement (Social psychology)
   USE   Alienation (Social psychology)

LC **Estrogen—Therapeutic use**
   NT   Estrogen replacement therapy

Estrogen replacement therapy
   BT   Estrogen—Therapeutic use
   RT   Hysterectomy
           Menopause

Ethnic groups
   USE   Minorities

Ethnic interadoption
   USE   Interethnic adoption

Ethnic intermarriage
   USE   Interethnic marriage

LC **Executives**
   BT   Business personnel
   NT   Executives, Women
   UF   Business executives
           Corporation executives

Executives, Women
   BT   Executives
   NT   Businesswomen
   UF   Business women
           Women executives
           Women in business

Extended family
   USE   Family, Extended

Extralegal marriage contracts
   USE   Marriage contracts, Extralegal

Extramarital relations
   cf.   note under ADULTERY
   BT   Sexuality
   RT   Homosexuality
           Marriage
           Prostitution
           Sexual freedom
   NT   Group sex
           Unmarried couples
   UF   ''Affairs'' (Amorous relationships)
           Comarital sex
           Consensual adultery
           Nonmarital relations
           Premarital relations
           Sex, Extramarital

Fair employment practice
   USE   Discrimination in employment

Fair housing
   USE   Discrimination in housing

Families of alcoholics
   USE   Alcoholism and the family

LC **Family**
   RT   Interpersonal relations
           Kinship
           Matriarchy
           Patriarchy
   NT   Alcoholism and the family
           Family alternatives
           Interethnic family
           Interracial family
           Interreligious family

NT   Single parent family
      headings beginning with the word FAMILY
UF   Family life
      Home life

Family, Alcoholism and the
 USE   Alcoholism and the family

Family, Communal
 USE   Communal family
      Communally organized groups

Family, Extended
 UF   Extended family

Family, Interethnic
 USE   Interethnic family

Family, Interracial
 USE   Interracial family

Family, Interreligious
 USE   Interreligious family

Family, Multiethnic
 USE   Interethnic family

Family, Multifaith
 USE   Interreligious family

Family, Multiracial
 USE   Interracial family

Family, Nuclear
 UF   Nuclear family

Family, One-parent
 USE   Single-parent family

Family, Single-parent
 USE   Single-parent family

Family, Transethnic
 USE   Interethnic family

Family, Transracial
 USE   Interracial family

Family alternatives
Here are entered works on nontraditional family organization including
works on non-blood related "family" groups. For works specifically on the
latter, see COMMUNAL LIFESTYLES.
 BT   Alternative life styles
      Family
 RT   Marriage alternatives
 NT   Child-free marriage
      Communal lifestyles
      Single-parent adoption
      Single-parent family

Family-career conflict, Women's
 USE   Women—Education—Role conflict
      Women—Employment—Role conflict

Family life
 USE   Family

Family networks
 USE   Communal family
      Communally organized groups

Family planning
 BT   Overpopulation
      Population control
 NT   Adoption
      Birth control
      Child-free marriage
 UF   Planned parenthood

Family planning and women's status
Here are entered works on the impact of family planning on women's potential place in society.
BT   Women—Social conditions
UF   Women's status and family planning

Farm laborers
USE   Agricultural workers

Farm workers
USE   Agricultural workers

LC **Farmers**
RT   Agriculturists
NT   Farmers, Women

Farmers, Women
BT   Farmers
RT   Agriculturists, Women
UF   Women farmers

Farmworkers
USE   Agricultural workers

LC **Fashion**
RT   Women's clothing

Father and child
BT   Parent and child
NT   Fathers and daughters
       Fathers and sons
UF   Child and father
       Father-child relationship

Father-child relationship
USE   Father and child

Father-separated children
BT   Parent-separated children
RT   Children of divorced parents
       Single mothers
       Single-parent family (Mother)
UF   Deprivation, Paternal
       Paternal deprivation

Fathers
BT   Men
       Parent and child
RT   Househusbands
NT   Homosexual fathers
       Parenting
       Single fathers
       Single-parent family (Father)
       Teen age fathers

Fathers, Homosexual
USE   Homosexual fathers

Fathers, Single
USE   Single fathers

Fathers, Unmarried
USE   Single fathers

Fathers, Unwed
USE   Single fathers

LC **Fathers and daughters**
BT   Father and child
UF   Daughters and fathers

LC **Fathers and sons**
BT   Father and child
UF   Sons and fathers

Female anatomy (Human)
USE   Human anatomy (Female)

The emerging woman; the impact of family planning. *(1970). "The purpose of this conference is . . . to brainstorm about the revolutionary changes in the role of women around the world due to the widespread use of contraceptives."*

LCSH makes a reference from Fashion *to* Men's Clothing.

LCSH: Paternal deprivation

Female cycles
  USE   Menopause
           Menstruation
Female homosexuality
  USE   Lesbianism
Female masturbation
  USE   Masturbation (Female)
Female orgasm
  USE   Orgasm (Female)
Female physiology (Human)
  USE   Human physiology (Female)
Female prostitutes
  USE   Prostitutes (Female)
Female sterilization (Human)
  USE   Sterilization of women (Birth control)
           Sterilization of women (Involuntary)
Female studies
  USE   Women's studies
Females
  USE   Women
Feminine mystique
  USE   Womanhood (Psychology)
Femininity (Psychology)
  USE   Womanhood (Psychology)
LC **Feminism (Indirect)**
  BT   Women—Civil rights
           Women—History
           Women—Legal status, laws, etc.
           Women—Social conditions
           Women's resistance and revolts
  RT   Sex discrimination
  NT   Women's movement (1960–   )
           subdivision FEMINIST PERSPECTIVE under topical subjects and
                   headings beginning with the words FEMINISM and FEMINIST
  UF   Women's rights feminism
Feminism—Biography
  USE   Feminists
Feminism—History
           To 500
           Middle ages, 500–1500
           Renaissance, 1450–1600
           Modern period, 1600–1900
           Twentieth century, 1900–
  BT   Women—History
  UF   Herstory

*The date subdivisions suggested apply
only to Western culture.*

Feminism—Library resources
  BT   Women—Library resources
Feminism—United States—History
           To 1848
           1848–1920
           1920–1960
           1960–
  NT   Women's movement (1960–   )—United States—History

Feminism—Great Britain [France,
Germany, etc.]—History. *Subdivide by
date as appropriate to the country, region, etc.*

Feminism, Anarchist
  BT   Anarchism and anarchists
           Feminism
  UF   Anarcha-feminism
           Anarchist feminism
Feminism, Christian
  RT   Judaeo-Christian religious tradition—Feminist perspective

Feminism, Christian (cont.)
UF   Christian feminism
        Christian feminists
        Christianity and feminism
        Feminism and Christianity

Feminism, Judaic
RT   Judaeo-Christian religious tradition—Feminist perspective
UF   Feminism and Judaism
        Jewish feminists
        Judaic feminism
        Judaism and feminism

Feminism, Lesbian
RT   Lesbians
UF   Feminism and lesbians
        Lesbian feminism
        Lesbians and feminism

Feminism, Marxist
USE   Feminism, Socialist

Feminism, Opposition to (Indirect)
UF   Anti-feminists

Feminism, Opposition to—History
Subdivide by date when appropriate as under FEMINISM—HISTORY.

Feminism, Radical
UF   Radical feminism

Feminism, Socialist
RT   Socialism and women; cf. note under SOCIALISM AND WOMEN
UF   Feminism, Marxist
        Marxist feminism
        Socialist feminism

Feminism and Christianity
USE   Feminism, Christian
        Judaeo-Christian religious tradition—Feminist perspective

Feminism and economic policy
USE   Economic policy—Feminist perspective

Feminism and employee training
USE   Employees, Training of—Feminist perspective

Feminism and employment (Part-time)
USE   Part-time employment—Feminist perspective

Feminism and human resources policy
USE   Human resources policy—Feminist perspective

Feminism and Jewish religious tradition
USE   Judaeo-Christian religious tradition—Feminist perspective

Feminism and Judaism
USE   Feminism, Judaic
        Judaeo-Christian religious tradition—Feminist perspective

Feminism and lesbians
USE   Feminism, Lesbian

Feminism and literature
USE   Literature—History and criticism—Feminist perspective

Feminism and occupational retraining
USE   Occupational retraining—Feminist perspective

Feminism and on the job training
USE   Employees, Training of—Feminist perspective

Feminism and pacifism
RT   Vietnamese conflict, 1961–1975—Protest movements, Women's
UF   Pacifism and feminism

Feminism and part-time employment
USE   Part-time employment—Feminist perspective

Feminism and progressivism (United States politics)
UF   Progressivism (United States politics) and feminism

Feminism and retraining (Occupational)
  USE   Occupational retraining—Feminist perspective

Feminism and the Judaeo-Christian religious tradition
  USE   Judaeo-Christian religious tradition—Feminist perspective

Feminism and training of employees
  USE   Employees, Training of—Feminist perspective

Feminism and volunteerism
  UF   Volunteer work and feminism
        Volunteerism and feminism

Feminism in literature
Here are entered works on the depiction of feminists and feminism in
literature. Feminist literary works are entered under FEMINIST LITERATURE.
  BT   Women in literature
  UF   Literature, Feminism in

Feminist counseling and therapy
  BT   Counseling
  RT   Counseling, Nonsexist
        Counseling for women
        Sexism in counseling
  NT   Feminist psychological counseling and therapy referral services
  UF   Counseling, Feminist
        Feminist therapy and counseling
        Therapy and counseling, Feminist

Feminist credit unions
  BT   Credit unions
        Women's projects and services
  RT   Banks and banking, Women's
        Sex discrimination in consumer credit
        Sex discrimination in mortgage loans
  UF   Credit unions, Feminist

Feminist economic policy
  USE   Economic policy—Feminist perspective

Feminist films
  BT   Women's films
  UF   Feminist motion pictures
        Films, Feminist
        Motion pictures, Feminist
        Moving pictures, Feminist

Feminist human resources policy
  USE   Human resources policy—Feminist perspective

Feminist literature
  cf.   note under FEMINISM IN LITERATURE
  NT   Feminist poetry
  UF   Literature, Feminist

Feminist literature—American [English, French, etc.] authors
  NT   Feminist poetry—American [English, French, etc.] authors
  UF   American literature—Feminist authors

Feminist magazines
  USE   Feminist periodicals

Feminist motion pictures
  USE   Feminist films

Feminist newspapers
  USE   Feminist periodicals

Feminist periodicals
  BT   Mass media, Women's
        Periodicals, Women's
  RT   Feminist publishers and publishing
  UF   Feminist magazines
        Feminist newspapers
        Magazines, Feminist

Feminist periodicals (cont.)
  UF   Newspapers, Feminist
       Periodicals, Feminist
Feminist poetry
  BT   Feminist literature
  UF   Poetry, Feminist
Feminist poetry—American [English, French, etc.] authors
  UF   American poetry—Feminist authors
Feminist politics
  UF   Politics, Feminist
Feminist psychoanalysis
  BT   Psychoanalysis
  RT   Sexism in psychoanalysis
  UF   Psychoanalysis, Feminist
Feminist psychological counseling and therapy referral services
  BT   Feminist psychotherapy
       Feminist counseling and therapy
       Women's projects and services
  UF   Feminist therapy referral services
       Psychological counseling and therapy referral services, Feminist
Feminist psychology
  BT   Psychology
  RT   Sexism in psychology
       Women—Psychology
  UF   Psychology, Feminist
Feminist psychotherapy
  BT   Psychotherapy
  RT   Sexism in psychotherapy
  NT   Feminist psychological counseling and therapy referral services
  UF   Psychotherapy, Feminist
Feminist publishers and publishing
  BT   Mass media, Women's
       Publishers and publishing
  RT   Feminist periodicals
       Women's presses
  UF   Publishers and publishing, Feminist
Feminist songs
  BT   Women—Songs and music
  UF   Songs, Feminist
Feminist spirituality
  NT   Feminist wicce and wicceans
  UF   Spirituality, Feminist
       Womanspirit
       Women—Spirituality
Feminist studies
  USE Women's studies
Feminist therapy and counseling
  USE Feminist counseling and therapy
Feminist therapy referral services
  USE Feminist psychological counseling and therapy referral services
Feminist vocational guidance
  BT   Vocational guidance
  RT   Sex-typing of occupations
       Sexism in vocational guidance
       Vocational guidance, Nonsexist
       Vocational guidance for women
  UF   Vocational guidance, Feminist
Feminist wicce and wicceans
Here are entered works on feminist witches and witchcraft.
  BT   Feminist spirituality

''The term witchcraft is derived from the Anglo-Saxon word wicce, meaning 'wise'— thus, 'wise-craft.' Its adherents

RT   Witchcraft
     Witches
UF   Feminist witchcraft and witches
     The craft, Feminism and
     The old religion, Feminism and
     Witchcraft and witches, Feminist
     Witches, Feminist

Feminist witchcraft and witches
USE   Feminist wicce and wicceans

Feminists
NT   Suffragists
     Women's movement (1960–)—Biography
     Women's movement (1960–)—Personal narratives
UF   Feminism—Biography

Fertility limitation, Human
USE   Population control

Field sports
USE   Sports

Film distributors, Women's
USE   Women's film distributors

Filmmakers
NT   Filmmakers, Women

Filmmakers, Women
BT   Filmmakers
     Mass media, Women's
RT   Women's film distributors
     Women's films
UF   Women filmmakers

Films
USE   Motion pictures

Films, Children's
USE   Children's films

Films, Feminist
USE   Feminist films

Films, Women's
USE   Women's films

Folklore of women
USE   Women in folklore and mythology

Forenames
USE   Names, Personal

Foster day care
USE   Child care
     Child care centers

LC   **Frontier and pioneer life (Indirect)**
RT   Pioneers
NT   Frontier and pioneer life of women
UF   Pioneer life

Frontier and pioneer life of women (Indirect)
BT   Frontier and pioneer life
RT   Pioneer women
UF   Women—Frontier and pioneer life
     Women pioneers

Fugitive slaves in the United States
USE   Slavery in the United States—Fugitive slaves

Funnies
USE   Comic books, strips, etc.

Gay authors
USE   Authors, Homosexual

Gay couples
USE   Homosexual couples

refer to it most commonly as wicce but also as the Craft, or the Old Religion.'' (The new woman's survival source-book, *1975. p. 197) The etymology is, quite possibly, incorrect.* The Oxford dictionary of English etymology *identifies wicce as the Anglo-Saxon form of witch and wis as the Anglo-Saxon form of wise. But whether the etymology is correct or not, the term in current usage among feminist wicceans is wicce.*

LCSH enters works on women pioneers under Frontier and pioneer life— United States [Australia, etc.] *and* Women—United States [Australia, etc.] *which makes it very difficult to find works on women pioneers.*

Gay couples (cont.)
USE   Homosexual couples (Men)
          Lesbian couples

Gay liberation Movement
BT   Social movements
RT   Homosexual men
          Lesbians
UF   Homophile movement
          Homosexual liberation movement

Gay lifestyle
USE   Homosexuality
          Homosexuals

Gay men
USE   Homosexual men

Gay parents
USE   Homosexual parents

Gay rights
USE   Homosexuals—Rights

Gay women
USE   Lesbians

Gays
USE   Homosexuals

Gender identity
USE   Sex (Psychology)
          Sex role

Gestation
USE   Pregnancy

Girl authors
USE   Authors, Girl

Girls (Indirect)
Here are entered works on women from the time of birth through age 12.
BT   Parent and child
          Women
NT   Juvenile delinquents (Female)

Girls—Counseling
USE   Counseling for girls

Girls—Crime
USE   Juvenile delinquents (Female)

Girls—Education (Indirect)   *LCSH:* Education of women
BT   Women—Education
RT   Primary Education—Curricula, Nonsexist
UF   Education—Girls

Girls—Occupation, Choice of
USE   Vocational guidance for girls

Girls—Rights
BT   Women—Civil rights
RT   Girls—Social conditions
UF   Girls' rights

Girls—Sex role socialization
USE   Sex role socialization of children

Girls—Sexuality
USE   Sexuality—Girls

Girls—Social conditions
BT   Women—Social conditions
RT   Girls—Rights

Girls—Vocational guidance
USE   Vocational guidance for girls

Girls—United States
NT   African-American [JEWISH-AMERICAN, MEXICAN-AMERICAN, etc.] girls

Girls, Counseling for
USE   Counseling for girls

Girls, Delinquent
USE   Juvenile delinquents (Female)

Girls' detention homes
USE   Juvenile detention homes (Female)

Girls' reformatories
USE   Reformatories (Female)

Girls' rights
USE   Girls—Rights

Government employment, Sex discrimination in
USE   Sex discrimination in government employment

Government officials
USE   Public officials

Grade school education
USE   Primary education

Graduate education
USE   Higher education—Graduate work

Graduate work
USE   Higher education—Graduate work

Grooming, Personal
NT   Grooming for men
        Grooming for women
UF   Personal grooming

LC **Grooming for men**
BT   Grooming, Personal
NT   Men's clothing
UF   Male grooming
        Men's grooming

Grooming for women
BT   Grooming, Personal
RT   Women's clothing
UF   Women's grooming

Group marriage
BT   Marriage alternatives
        Polygamy
        Sexual freedom
UF   Marriage, Group

LC **Group sex**
BT   Extramarital relations
        Sexual freedom
NT   Swinging and swingers (Sex customs)
UF   Orgies

Guidance, Student
USE   Vocational guidance

Guidance, Vocational
USE   Vocational guidance

LC **Gynecology**
RT   Women—Diseases
NT   Sexism in gynecology

Gynecology—Popular works

Gynecology, Sexism in
USE   Sexism in gynecology

Hatred of men
RT   Misogyny
UF   Androphobia

Hatred of women
USE   Misogyny

LCSH: Beauty, Personal. *We aren't all beautiful!*

Headings, Subject
  USE   Subject headings

Health   *LCSH:* Hygiene
  RT   Mental health
  NT   subdivision HEALTH under headings for classes of persons; e.g.
             MEN—HEALTH; MIDDLE AGE WOMEN—HEALTH; TEEN AGE
             WOMEN—HEALTH; WOMEN—HEALTH, etc.
  UF   Hygiene

Health care
  USE   Medical care

Health centers, Women's
  USE   Women's health centers and clinics

Health personnel
  USE   Medical personnel

Health sciences personnel
  USE   Medical personnel

Health services
  USE   Medical care

Heroines in literature
  USE   Women in folklore and mythology
         Women in literature

Herstory
  USE   Feminism—History
  USE   Women—History

Heterosexual marriage
  USE   Marriage (Heterosexual)

Heterosexuality
  BT   Sexuality

High School education
  USE   Secondary education

Higher education   *LCSH:* Education, Higher
Here are entered general works on higher education. Works on the
physical plants and on the administration of universities and colleges are
entered under UNIVERSITIES AND COLLEGES.
  BT   Education
  RT   Universities and colleges
  NT   Women—Higher education
  UF   Education, Higher

Higher education—Curricula   *LCSH: establishes both* Education,
  BT   Education—Curricula   Higher—Curricula *and* Universities
  NT   Higher Education—Honors courses   and colleges—Curricula; *its entries for*
  UF   Universities and colleges—Curricula   Graduate work *and* Honors courses
                                                                        are established as subdivisions under
Higher education—Curricula, Nonsexist   Universities and colleges *rather than*
  RT   Sexism in curricula (Higher education)   *under* Higher education. *It is recom-*
        Women—Higher education   *mended that the heading* Universities
        Women's studies   and colleges *be used only for works on*
  UF   Higher education—Nonsexist curricula   *the physical plant and the administra-*
                                                                        tion of universities and colleges with
Higher education—Graduate work   *subdivisions such as* Accreditation, Ad-
  NT   Women—Higher education—Graduate work   ministration buildings, Finance, *etc.*
  UF   Graduate education   *Works about higher education itself*
        Graduate work   *should be entered under* Higher educa-
        Post graduate work   tion *with appropriate subdivision.*

Higher education—Honors courses
  BT   Higher education—Curricula
  NT   Women—Higher education—Honors courses
  UF   Honors courses in college
        Honors work in college

Higher education—Nonsexist curricula
  USE   Higher education—Curricula, Nonsexist

Higher education—Sexism in curricula
  USE   Sexism in curricula (Higher education)

Higher education—Women
  USE   Women—Higher education

Hispano women
  USE   Latino women—United States

Historians, Women
    cf.   note under WOMEN IN HISTORIOGRAPHY
    UF   Women historians

Historiography, Women in
  USE   Women in historiography

History, Women in
  USE   Women in historiography

Home childbirth
  USE   Childbirth at home

Home life
  USE   Family

Home violence
  USE   Household violence

Homemakers
    NT   Househusbands
           Housewives

Homemakers (Paid workers)
  USE   Household workers

Homophile movement
  USE   Gay liberation movement

Homophiles
  USE   Homosexuals

Homophobia
    BT   Discrimination
    RT   Homosexuals
    NT   Homosexuality and employment
    UF   Discrimination against Gays
           Discrimination against homosexuals
           Homosexuals—Discrimination

Homophobia in subject headings
    BT   Subject headings
    RT   Subject headings—Homosexuals and homosexuality
    UF   Subject headings, Homophobia in

Homosexual actors and actresses
  USE   Actors and actresses, Homosexual

Homosexual authors
  USE   Authors, Homosexual

Homosexual couples
    RT   Marriage (Homosexual)
    NT   Homosexual couples (Men)
           Lesbian couples
    UF   Couples, Homosexual
           Gay couples

Homosexual couples (Men)
    BT   Homosexual couples
    UF   Gay couples

Homosexual couples (Women)
  USE   Lesbian couples

Homosexual fathers
    BT   Fathers
           Homosexual parents
    RT   Homosexual men and child custody
    UF   Fathers, Homosexual

Homosexual liberation movement
  USE   Gay liberation movement

Homosexual marriage
  USE   Marriage (Homosexual)

Homosexual Men
    BT   Homosexuals
           Men
    RT   Gay liberation movement
           headings beginning with the words HOMOSEXUAL MEN and
               HOMOSEXUAL
    UF   Gay men
           Men homosexuals

Homosexual men—Legal status, laws, etc.
    BT   Homosexuals—Legal status, laws, etc.
    NT   Homosexual men and child custody

Homosexual men—Psychology
    BT   Men—Psychology
    RT   Homosexuality (Male)

Homosexual men and child custody
    BT   Child custody
           Homosexual men—Legal status, laws, etc.
           Men and child custody
    RT   Homosexual fathers
           Homosexual men in heterosexual marriage
    UF   Child custody and homosexual men

Homosexual men authors
  USE   Authors, Homosexual men

Homosexual men in heterosexual marriage
    BT   Homosexuals in heterosexual marriage
    RT   Homosexual men and child custody
    UF   Marriage (Heterosexual), Homosexual men in

Homosexual men in literature
    BT   Homosexuals in literature; cf. note under HOMOSEXUALS IN
               LITERATURE
    UF   Literature, Homosexual men in

Homosexual men in motion pictures
    BT   Homosexuals in motion pictures; cf. note under HOMOSEXUALS IN
               MOTION PICTURES
    UF   Motion pictures, Homosexual men in

Homosexual parents
    BT   Parent and child
    RT   Children of homosexual parents
    NT   Homosexual fathers
           Lesbian mothers
    UF   Gay parents
           Parents, Homosexual

Homosexual parents, Children of
  USE   Children of homosexual parents

Homosexual women
  USE   Lesbians

LC **Homosexuality**
Here are entered works on medical and psychological research exclusive
of case studies. Works on homosexuals themselves, including case studies,
are entered under HOMOSEXUALS.
    BT   Sexuality
    RT   Homosexuals
    NT   Homosexuality (Male)
           Lesbianism
    UF   Gay lifestyle
           Same-sex lifestyle

Homosexuality—Law and legislation
    BT   Sex and law

RT   Homosexuals—Legal status, laws, etc.
   Homosexuals—Rights

Homosexuality—Subject headings
 USE   Subject headings—Homosexuals and homosexuality

Homosexuality (Female)
 USE   Lesbianism

Homosexuality (Male)
 BT   Homosexuality
   Sexuality—Men
 RT   Homosexual men—Psychology
 UF   Male homosexuality
   Men—Homosexuality

LC **Homosexuality and employment**
 BT   Discrimination in employment
   Homophobia
 UF   Employment and homosexuality

Homosexuals
Here are entered works on homosexuals including case studies. Works on
medical and psychological research, exclusive of case studies, are entered
under HOMOSEXUALITY.
 RT   Extramarital relations
   Homophobia
   Homosexuality
 NT   Homosexual men
   Lesbians
   headings beginning with the words HOMOSEXUAL, HOMOSEXUALS,
    LESBIAN, and LESBIANS
 UF   Gay lifestyle
   Gays
   Homophiles
   Same-sex lifestyle

Homosexuals—Discrimination
 USE   Homophobia

Homosexuals—Legal status, laws, etc.
 RT   Homosexuality—Law and legislation
   Homosexuals—Rights
 NT   Homosexual men—Legal status, laws, etc.
   Lesbians—Legal status, laws, etc.

Homosexuals—Rights
 RT   Homosexuality—Law and legislation
   Homosexuals—Legal status, laws, etc.
 UF   Gay rights

Homosexuals—Subject headings
 USE   Subject headings—Homosexuals and homosexuality

Homosexuals in heterosexual marriage
 BT   Marriage (Heterosexual)
 NT   Homosexual men in heterosexual marriage
   Lesbians in heterosexual marriage
 UF   Marriage (Heterosexual), Homosexuals in

Homosexuals in literature
Here are entered works on the representation of homosexuals in literature.
Works on homosexual authors are entered under AUTHORS, HOMOSEXUAL.
 NT   Homosexual men in literature
   Lesbians in literature
 UF   Literature, Homosexuals in

Homosexuals in motion pictures
Here are entered works on the depiction of homosexuals in motion
pictures. Works on homosexual actors and actresses are entered under
ACTORS AND ACTRESSES, HOMOSEXUAL.
 BT   Motion pictures
 NT   Homosexual men in motion pictures

Homosexuals in motion pictures (cont.)
   NT   Lesbians in motion pictures
   UF   Motion pictures, Homosexuals in

Honors courses in college
  USE   Higher education—Honors courses

Honors work in college
  USE   Higher education—Honors courses

Hookers
  USE   Prostitutes

Household violence
   BT   Violence
   NT   Child battering
           Woman battering
   UF   Home violence
           Violence, Household
           Violence in the home

Household workers   *LCSH:* Servants
   BT   Working classes—Employment
   RT   Household workers' movement
           Wages—Household workers
   NT   Household workers, Women
   UF   Day workers (Domestic)
           Domestic workers
           Domestics
           Homemakers (Paid workers)
           Housekeepers, Paid
           Private household workers
           Servants
           Workers, Domestic

Household workers, Women
   BT   Household workers
           Working class women—Employment
   UF   Cleaning women
           Housemaids
           Maids
           Women day workers (Domestic)
           Women domestics
           Women household workers

Household workers' movement
   RT   Household workers

Househusbands
   BT   Homemakers
   RT   Fathers
           Married men

Housekeepers, Paid
  USE   Household workers

Housemaids
  USE   Household workers, Women

LC **Housewives**
   BT   Homemakers
   RT   Married women
           Mothers
           Wages for housework movement

Housework movement, Wages for
  USE   Wages for housework movement

Housing, Discrimination in housing
  USE   Discrimination in housing

Housing, Sex discrimination in housing
  USE   Sex discrimination in housing

Human anatomy   *LCSH:* Anatomy, Human
   BT   Human physiology
   UF   Anatomy, Human

Human anatomy (Female)
UF   Anatomy, Female (Human)
      Female anatomy (Human)
      Women—Anatomy

Human anatomy (Male)
UF   Anatomy, Male (Human)
      Male anatomy (Human)
      Men—Anatomy

Human artificial impregnation
USE   Artificial insemination, Human

Human artificial insemination
USE   Artificial insemination, Human

Human birth
USE   Childbirth

Human evolution—Feminist perspective

Human fertility limitation
USE   Population control

LC **Human physiology**
NT   Human anatomy
UF   Physiology, Human

Human physiology (Female)
UF   Female physiology (Human)
      Physiology, Female (Human)
      Women—Physiology

Human physiology (Male)
UF   Male physiology (Human)
      Men—Physiology
      Physiology, Male (Human)

Human relations
USE   Interpersonal relations

Human resources
RT   Labor supply
UF   Manpower
      Womanpower

Human resources development
USE   Human resources policy

Human resources policy
BT   Economic policy
RT   Labor supply
NT   Occupational retraining
      Occupational training
      Vocational education
UF   Human resources development
      Human resources utilization

Human resources policy—Feminist perspective
Here are entered works on the changes in the organization of the worlds of
education and employment (e.g. provision for flexible school and work
hours and weeks, convenient and rewarding part-time schooling and employment, convenient and competent day care, nondiscriminatory maternity and child care leaves, wages, pensions, etc.) and in the attitudes of
society towards women's equal participation in the world of work that are
a necessary preliminary to equal employment opportunity for women.
BT   Economic policy—Feminist perspective
RT   Women—Social conditions
NT   Educational opportunity and women's status
      subdivision FEMINIST PERSPECTIVE under CHILD CARE, PART-TIME
        EMPLOYMENT and similar headings; also subdivision HUMAN
        RESOURCES POLICY—FEMINIST PERSPECTIVE under names of
        countries, regions, cities, etc.

Human resources utilization
USE   Human resources policy

LCSH formerly had a heading Woman
—Anatomy and physiology. *General
works and works on male anatomy
were entered under* Anatomy, Human;
*works on female anatomy were entered
under the heading above. In response
to criticism for thus splitting the material (and, by implication, attributing a
somewhat less than human status to
women), they dropped the* Woman—
Anatomy . . . *heading and now enter
all works under* Anatomy, Human,
*which is not an adequate solution to
the problem. There are works specifically on female, or on male, anatomy.
Library users interested only in female,
or only in male, anatomy should be as-
sisted in distinguishing specific works
from general works. See also* Human
physiology *below where the same problem existed and the same inadequate
solution was applied.*

LCSH: Manpower

Human rights
USE   Civil rights

Human sexuality
USE   Sexuality

LC **Husband and wife**
Here are entered general works on legal relations between husband and wife. Works on the effect of marriage on women's legal capacity are entered under MARRIED WOMEN—LEGAL STATUS, LAWS, ETC. Works on the effect of marriage on men's legal responsibilities are entered under MARRIED MEN—LEGAL STATUS, LAWS, ETC. General works on married people are entered under MARRIED PEOPLE.
RT   Married men—Legal status, laws, etc.
        Married people
        Married women—Legal status, laws, etc.
UF   Wife and husband

Husbands
USE   Married men

Husbands, Runaway
USE   Runaway wives, husbands, etc.

Hygiene
USE   Health

Hygiene, Mental
USE   Mental health

Hymns (Christian), Nonsexist
UF   Nonsexist hymns, Christian

Hysterectomy
BT   Sterilization of women (Birth control)
        Sterilization of women (Involuntary)
RT   Estrogen replacement therapy

I U D
USE   Intrauterine contraceptives

I. W. D.
USE   International Women's Day
        International Women's Decade

I. W. Y.
USE   International Women's Year

In-service training
USE   Employees, Training of

Indexing vocabularies
USE   Subject headings

Induced abortion
USE   Abortion

Induced labor (Childbirth)
USE   Childbirth—Labor, Induced

Industrial law
USE   Labor laws and legislation

Inebriates
USE   Alcoholics

Infant school
USE   Preschool education

Insemination, Artificial (Human)
USE   Artificial insemination, Human

Instruction
USE   Education

Instructional materials
USE   Teaching materials

Insurance, social
USE   Social security

Insurance, State and compulsory
USE   Social security

Emswiler, Sharon Neufer. Women and worship; a guide to non-sexist hymns, prayers, and liturgies (1974). LC assigned: Liturgies, Public worship, and Women in Christianity; all of which are vague and the last totally inappropriate. The use of Hymns (Christian), Nonsexist, Liturgies (Christian), Nonsexist, and Prayers (Christian), Nonsexist is recommended. (The unglossed LCSH form of "hymns," "liturgies," and "prayers" is, by the way, a good example of the Christian bias of the LCSH.)

Intentional abortion
  USE   Abortion

Interadoption
Here are entered general works on the adoption of children of different
religions, religious denominations, nationalities, races, and/or ethnic groups
from that of the adopting parent or parents. Works on specific forms of
interadoption are entered under the appropriate specific heading; e.g.
INTERRACIAL ADOPTION, INTERRELIGIOUS ADOPTION.
  BT   Adoption
  NT   Interethnic adoption
        International adoption
        Interracial adoption
        Interreligious adoption
  UF   Adoption, Mixed
        Mixed adoption

Intercountry adoption
  USE   International adoption

Interethnic adoption
  BT   Interadoption
  RT   Interethnic family
  UF   Adoption, Interethnic
        Adoption, Transethnic
        Ethnic interadoption
        Transethnic adoption

Interethnic family
  BT   Family
  RT   Interethnic adoption
        Interethnic marriage
  UF   Family, Interethnic
        Family, Multiethnic
        Family, Transethnic
        Multiethnic family
        Transethnic family

Interethnic marriage
  BT   Intermarriage
  RT   Interethnic family
  UF   Ethnic intermarriage
        Marriage, Interethnic
        Marriage, Transethnic
        Transethnic marriage

Interfaith adoption
  USE   Interreligious adoption

Interfaith family
  USE   Interreligious family

Interfaith marriage
  USE   Interreligious marriage

Intermarriage
Here are entered general works on marriage between persons of different
religions, religious denominations, races, and/or ethnic groups. Works on
specific forms of intermarriage are entered under the appropriate specific
heading; e.g. INTERRELIGIOUS MARRIAGE, INTERRACIAL MARRIAGE, etc.
  BT   Marriage
  NT   Interethnic marriage
        Interracial marriage
        Interreligious marriage
  UF   Marriage, Mixed
        Mixed marriage

International adoption
Here are entered general works on the adoption of children across national
boundaries. General works on the adoption of children of different religions, religious denominations, nationalities, races, and/or ethnic groups
from that of the adopting parent or parents are entered under INTER-
ADOPTION.

International adoption (cont.)
   BT   Interadoption
   UF   Adoption, International
          Intercountry adoption
          Transnational adoption

International Women's Day
   UF   I. W. D.
          Women's Day, International

International Women's Decade
   UF   I. W. D.
          Women's Decade, International

International Women's Year
   UF   I. W. Y.
          Women's Year, International

LC **Interpersonal relations**
   RT   Children and parents
          Family
          Parent and child
   NT   Interpersonal relations, Nonsexist
          Interpersonal relations in marriage
          Sexism in interpersonal relations
   UF   Human relations

Interpersonal relations, Nonsexist
   BT   Interpersonal relations
   RT   Sexism in interpersonal relations
   NT   Interpersonal relations in marriage, Nonsexist
   UF   Nonsexist interpersonal relations

Interpersonal relations, Sexism in
   USE   Sexism in interpersonal relations

Interpersonal relations in marriage
   BT   Interpersonal relations
   NT   Wife-beating
   UF   Marriage—Human relations
          Marriage—Interpersonal relations

Interpersonal relations in marriage, Nonsexist
   BT   Interpersonal relations, Nonsexist
   UF   Marriage, Nonsexist
          Nonsexist marriage

Interracial adoption
   BT   Interadoption
   RT   Interracial family
   UF   Adoption, Interracial
          Adoption, Transracial
          Racial interadoption
          Transracial adoption

Interracial family
   BT   Family
   RT   Interracial adoption
          Interracial marriage
   UF   Family, Interracial
          Family, Multiracial
          Family, Transracial
          Multiracial family
          Transracial family

LC **Interracial marriage**
   BT   Intermarriage
   RT   Interracial family
   UF   Marriage, Interracial
          Marriage, Transracial
          Racial intermarriage
          Transracial marriage

Interreligious adoption
  BT   Interadoption
  RT   Interreligious family
  UF   Adoption, Interfaith
        Adoption, Interreligious
        Interfaith adoption
        Religious interadoption

Interreligious family
  BT   Family
  RT   Interreligious adoption
        Interreligious marriage
  UF   Family, Interfaith
        Family, Interreligious
        Family, Multifaith
        Interfaith family
        Multifaith family

Interreligious marriage   *LCSH:* Marriage, Mixed
  BT   Intermarriage
  RT   Interreligious family
  UF   Interfaith marriage
        Marriage, Interfaith
        Marriage, Interreligious
        Religious intermarriage

LC **Intrauterine contraceptives**
  BT   Contraceptives
  UF   Coil (Birth control device)
        I U D
        IUD
        Loop (Birth control device)
        Shield (Birth control device)

Intrauterine contraceptives—Effectiveness

Intrauterine contraceptives—Mental and physiological effects
  UF   Intrauterine contraceptives—Physiological effects
        Intrauterine contraception—Psychological aspects

Intrauterine contraceptives—Physiological effects
  USE   Intrauterine contraceptives—Mental and physiological effects

Intrauterine contraceptives—Psychological aspects
  USE   Intrauterine contraceptives—Mental and physiological effects

IUD
  USE   Intrauterine contraceptives

Jails
  USE   Prisons

Jewish-American women
  BT   Jewish women
        Minority women—United States
  RT   Jewish women—United States
  UF   Women, Jewish-American

Jewish-American women—Education

Jewish-American women's organizations
  BT   Women's organizations—United States

Jewish feminists
  USE   Feminism, Judaic

Jewish cantors
  USE   Cantors (Jewish)

Jewish life (Religious)
  USE   Religious life (Judaism)

Jewish rabbis
  USE   Rabbis

Jewish religious tradition and feminism
  USE   Judaeo-Christian religious tradition—Feminist perspective

Jewish teen age women
    BT   Jewish women
          Teen age women
    UF   Teen age women, Jewish

Jewish teen age women—Religious life
    NT   Bas Mitzvah

Jewish way of life
    USE   Jews—Social life and customs

Jewish women (Indirect)
    BT   Women
    RT   Judaism and women
    NT   Jewish-American women
          Jewish teen age women
    UF   Women, Jewish

Jewish women—United States
Here are entered works on Jewish women residing in the United States who are not citizens. Works on Jewish women who are citizens are entered under JEWISH-AMERICAN WOMEN.
    RT   Jewish-American women

Jewish women cantors
    USE   Cantors, Women (Jewish)

LC **Jews—Social life and customs**
    NT   Religious life (Judaism)
    UF   Jewish way of life
          Life, Jewish way of
          Way of life, Jewish

Job discrimination
    USE   Discrimination in employment

Job hunting
    RT   Employment agencies
          Employment interviewing
    NT   Job hunting for women

Job hunting for women
    BT   Job hunting
    RT   Affirmative action organizations, centers, etc.
          Employment interviewing, Nonsexist
          Sexism in employment interviewing

Job interviewing
    USE   Employment interviewing

Job placement services
    USE   Employment agencies

Job retraining
    USE   Occupational retraining

LC **Job satisfaction**
    BT   Attitude (Psychology)
    NT   Absenteeism (Labor)
          Women—Employment—Job satisfaction

Job-sharing
    RT   Part-time employment
    UF   Employment, Part-time
          Part-time work

Job training
    USE   Occupational training

Jobs
    USE   Occupations
          Professions
          Vocational guidance

Judaeo-Christian religious tradition—Feminist perspective
Here are entered feminist works which reevaluate the traditional

LCSH: Jewish way of life. *The LCSH heading is assigned to works on Jewish religious life and to works on Jewish customs and traditions.* Social life and customs *is a standard LCSH subdivision for use under names of peoples, and its use is recommended rather than the vague* Jewish way of life.

interpretation of women's role in Biblical events and works on the effect of
that traditional interpretation on the place of women in society.

    RT   Christianity and women
           Feminism, Christian
           Feminism, Judaic
           Judaism and women
    UF   Christian religious tradition and feminism
           Christianity and feminism
           Feminism and Christianity
           Feminism and Jewish religious tradition
           Feminism and Judaism
           Feminism and the Judaeo-Christian religious tradition
           Jewish religious tradition and feminism
           Judaism and feminism

Judaic feminism
  USE   Feminism, Judaic

Judaism and feminism
  USE   Feminism, Judaic
           Judaeo-Christian religious tradition—Feminist perspective

Judaism and women
Here are entered works on the status of women in the Jewish tradition.
For works on the theological position of women in Judaism see WOMAN
(JEWISH THEOLOGY). For works on the day-to-day religious practice of
Jewish women see RELIGIOUS LIFE (JUDAISM)—WOMEN.

    BT   Religion and women
    RT   Jewish women
           Judeo-Christian religious tradition—Feminist perspective
           Religious life (Judaism)—Women
           Woman (Jewish theology)
    UF   Women and Judaism
           Women in Judaism

LC **Juvenile delinquency**
Here are entered works on juvenile delinquency as a social problem
including works on public opinion, research, statistics, and efforts to
combat it. Works on delinquents themselves, including case studies and
personal narratives, are entered under JUVENILE DELINQUENTS.

    BT   Crime and criminals
    RT   Juvenile delinquents
           Juvenile detention homes
           Reformatories
    UF   Delinquency, Juvenile

Juvenile delinquents
    RT   Juvenile delinquency; cf. note under JUVENILE DELINQUENCY
    NT   Prostitutes, Child
    UF   Delinquency, Juvenile
           Delinquents, Juvenile

LCSH: Juvenile delinquency.

Juvenile delinquents (Female)
    BT   Criminals, Women
           Girls
           Teen age women
    UF   Girls—Crime
           Girls, Delinquent
           Teen age women—Crime
           Teen age women, Delinquent

LCSH: Delinquent girls. *The LCSH reference from* Delinquent girls *to* Unmarried mothers *is jarring; ''girls'' are seldom mothers—at least in our climate.*

Juvenile delinquents (Male)
    BT   Boys
           Criminals, Men
           Teen age men
    UF   Boys—Crime
           Boys, Delinquent
           Teen age men—Crime
           Teen age men, Delinquent

LCSH: Juvenile delinquency.

LC **Juvenile detention homes**
 RT Juvenile delinquency
   Reformatories
 NT Juvenile detention homes (Female)
   Juvenile detention homes (Male)
 UF Children's prisons
   Detention homes, Juvenile
   Remand homes

Juvenile detention homes (Female)
 UF Girls' detention homes

Juvenile detention homes (Male)
 UF Boys' detention homes

Juvenile film
 USE Children's films

Juvenile literature
 USE Children's literature

Kinship
 RT Family
 NT Matrilineal kinship
   Patrilineal kinship

Labor (Childbirth)
 USE Childbirth—Labor

Labor, Painless (Childbirth)
 USE Lamaze technique (Childbirth)

Labor absenteeism
 USE Absenteeism (Labor)

Labor force
 USE Labor supply

LC **Labor laws and legislation**
 NT Discrimination in employment—Law and legislation
   Labor laws and legislation, Discriminatory
 UF Industrial law
   Law, Industrial
   Law, Labor

Labor laws and legislation—Women
 BT Women—Legal status, laws, etc.
 RT Women—Employment—Legal aspects
 NT Affirmative action for women
   Labor laws and legislation, Discriminatory—Women
   Sex discrimination in employment—Law and legislation
 UF Women—Employment—Law and Legislation

Labor laws and legislation, Discriminatory
 BT Labor laws and legislation
 UF Discrimination in labor laws and legislation

Labor laws and legislation, Discriminatory—Women
 BT Labor laws and legislation—Women
   Women—Legal status, laws, etc.—Discriminatory legislation
 UF Sex discrimination in labor laws and legislation

Labor market
 USE Labor supply

LC **Labor supply**
 BT Economic policy
 RT Human resources
   Human resources policy
 NT LABOR SUPPLY (TEEN AGE); LABOR SUPLY (WOMEN) and similar headings
 UF Labor force
   Labor market
   Unemployment

LCSH uses Women—Employment, Youth—Employment, *and similar nonspecific headings for works on the number of women in the labor force, potentially in the labor force, unable to*

Labor supply (Teen age)
- RT   Teen age—Employment
-       Teen age and employment
- UF   Teen age and unemployment
-       Teen agers in the labor force
-       Teen agers in the labor market
-       Unemployment and teen age

Labor supply (Women)
- RT   Women—Employment
- UF   Unemployment and women
-       Women and unemployment
-       Women in the labor force
-       Women in the labor market

Labor unionists, Women
- BT   Labor unions
- RT   Sex discrimination in labor unions
-       Sexism in labor unions
-       Working class women—Employment
- UF   Women labor unionists
-       Women trade unionists

Labor unions
- RT   Professional unions
-       Workers
- NT   Labor unionists, Women
- UF   Trade unions
-       Unions, Labor
-       Unions, White collar
-       White collar unions

Labor unions, Sex discrimination in
- USE   Sex discrimination in labor unions

Labor unions, Sexism in
- USE   Sexism in labor unions

Laborers
- USE   Working classes—Employment

Laboring classes
- USE   Working classes

Lamaze technique (Childbirth)
- BT   Natural childbirth
- UF   Labor, Painless (Childbirth)
-       Lemaze technique (Childbirth)
-       Painless labor (Childbirth)
-       Psychoprophylactic childbirth

Language and sex role
- USE   Sex role and language
-       Sexism in language (English)

Laparoscopic tubal coagulation
- USE   Laparoscopy

LC **Laparoscopy**
- BT   Sterilization of women (Birth control)
- RT   Tubal ligation (Birth control)
- UF   Laparoscopic tubal coagulation

Latinas—United States
- USE   Latino women—United States

Latino women—United States
- BT   Minority women—United States
- NT   Mexican-American women
-       Puerto Rican-American women
- UF   Chicanas
-       Chicano women
-       Hispano women

gain entry into the labor force or unable to gain entry at the level for which they are qualified. Works on the labor supply of persons of specific ages and/or sex should be entered under Labor supply *with an appropriate gloss.*

LCSH: Women in trade-unions

LCSH: Trade-unions

Latino women—United States (cont.)
  UF   Latinas
          Spanish-American women—United States

Law, Industrial
  USE   Labor laws and legislation

Law, Labor
  USE   Labor laws and legislation

Law, Sex discrimination in
  USE   Women—Legal status, laws, etc.—Discriminatory legislation

Law and sex
  USE   Sex and law

Law paraprofessionals
  BT   Paraprofessions and paraprofessionals
  NT   Law paraprofessionals, Women
  UF   Legal paraprofessionals

Law paraprofessionals, Women
  BT   Law paraprofessionals
  UF   Women law paraprofessionals
          Women legal paraprofessionals

Learned periodicals
  USE   Scholarly periodicals

LC **Leave of absence (Employment)**
  NT   Child care leave
          Maternity leave
  UF   Absence, Leave of (Employment)

Legal paraprofessionals
  USE   Law paraprofessionals

Legal status of women
  USE   Women—Legal status, laws, etc.

LC **Legislators (Indirect)**
  NT   Legislators, Women

LC **Legislators—United States**
  NT   Legislators, Women—United States
  UF   Congressmen and women

Legislators, Women (Indirect)
  BT   Politicians, Women
  UF   Women legislators

Legislators, Women—United States
  NT   Congresswomen (House)
          Senators (United States), Women

Lemaze technique (Childbirth)
  USE   Lamaze technique (Childbirth)

Lesbian authors
  USE   Authors, Lesbian

Lesbian couples
  BT   Homosexual couples
  UF   Couples, Lesbian
          Gay couples
          Homosexual couples (Women)

Lesbian feminism
  USE   Feminism, Lesbian

Lesbian mothers
  BT   Homosexual parents
          Mothers
  RT   Lesbians and child custody
  UF   Mothers, Lesbian

Lesbianism
  BT   Homosexuality
          Sexuality—Women

RT   Lesbians—Psychology
UF   Female homosexuality
       Homosexuality (Female)
       Women—Homosexuality

Lesbians
    BT   Homosexuals
          Women
    RT   Gay liberation movement
          headings beginning with the words LESBIAN and LESBIANS
    UF   Gay women
          Homosexual women
          Women homosexuals

Lesbians—Legal status, laws, etc.
    BT   Homosexuals—Legal status, laws, etc.
          Lesbians—Social conditions
          Women—Legal status, laws, etc.
    NT   Lesbians and child custody

Lesbians—Psychology
    BT   Women—Psychology
    RT   Lesbianism

Lesbians—Social conditions
    BT   Women—Social conditions
    NT   Lesbians—Legal status, laws, etc.

Lesbians and child custody
    BT   Child custody
          Lesbian—Legal status, laws, etc.
          Women and child custody
    RT   Lesbian mothers
          Lesbians in heterosexual marriage
    UF   Child custody and lesbians

Lesbians and feminism
    USE   Feminism, Lesbian

Lesbians in heterosexual marriage
    BT   Homosexuals in heterosexual marriage
    RT   Lesbians and child custody
    UF   Marriage (Heterosexual), Lesbians in

Lesbians in literature
Here are entered works on the representation of lesbians in literature.
Works on lesbian authors are entered under AUTHORS, LESBIAN.
    BT   Homosexuals in literature
          Women in literature
    UF   Literature, Lesbians in

Lesbians in motion pictures
    BT   Homosexuals in motion pictures; cf. note under HOMOSEXUALS IN
             MOTION PICTURES
          Women in motion pictures
    UF   Motion pictures, Lesbians in

Librarians, Women
    BT   Professional women
    UF   Women librarians

LC **Librarians' unions**
    BT   Professional unions

LC **Library resources**
Here are entered works describing the resources and special collections in
libraries which are available for research in various fields. Works describing the resources and special collections in a particular field are entered under the subject with subdivision LIBRARY RESOURCES; e.g. FEMINISM—
LIBRARY RESOURCES; WOMEN—LIBRARY RESOURCES.

Library technicians
    BT   Paraprofessions and paraprofessionals

Library technicians (cont.)
NT   Library technicians, Women
UF   Paraprofessions and paraprofessionals—Librarianship

Library technicians, Women
BT   Library technicians
UF   Women library technicians

Life, Jewish way of
USE   Jews—Social life and customs

Life at sea
USE   Sailors

Life-long education
USE   Adult education

Lifestyles, Alternative
USE   Alternative lifestyles

Lifestyles, Communal
USE   Communal lifestyles

Literature—History and criticism—Feminist perspective
RT   Sex role in literature
NT   American literature—History and criticism—Feminist perspective
English literature—History and criticism—Feminist perspective
UF   Feminism and literature
Literature and feminism

Literature, Feminism in
USE   Feminism in literature

Literature, Feminist
USE   Feminist literature

Literature, Homosexuals in
USE   Homosexuals in literature

Literature, Lesbians in
USE   Lesbians in literature

Literature, Misogyny in
USE   Misogyny in literature

Literature, Sex role in
USE   Sex role in literature

Literature, Women in
USE   Women in literature

Literature and feminism
USE   Literature—History and criticism—Feminist perspective

Little presses
USE   Small presses

Liturgies (Christian), Nonsexist
UF   Nonsexist liturgies (Christian)

LC **Local officials and employees**
BT   Public officials
RT   State governments—Officials and employees

Local officials and employees, Women
BT   Women—Employment
UF   Women local officials and employees

Loop (Birth control device)
USE   Intrauterine contraceptives

Lumpectomy
USE   Breast cancer—Surgery

Magazines
USE   Periodicals

Magazines, Feminist
USE   Feminist periodicals

Magazines, Women's
USE   Periodicals, Women's

Emswiler, Sharon Neufer. Women and worship; a guide to non-sexist hymns, prayers, and liturgies *(1974)*

Maids
USE   Household workers, Women

Male anatomy (Human)
USE   Human anatomy (Male)

Male grooming
USE   Grooming for men

Male homosexuality
USE   Homosexuality (Male)

Male masturbation
USE   Masturbation (Male)

Male orgasm
USE   Orgasm (Male)

Male physiology (Human)
USE   Human physiology (Male)

Male prostitutes
USE   Prostitutes (Male)

Male sterilization (Human)
USE   Sterilization of men (Birth control)

"Mammies" (Slavery in the United States)
USE   Slavery in the United States—Treatment of women household
            slaves

Mammography
  BT   Breast examination
  UF   Breast radiography

Man (Christian theology)
  BT   Man (Theology)
          Man and woman (Christian theology)

Man (Jewish theology)
  BT   Man (Theology)
          Man and woman (Jewish theology)

Man (Theology)
  BT   Man and woman (Theology)
  NT   Man (Christian theology)
          Man (Jewish theology)

Man and woman (Christian theology)
  BT   Man and woman (Theology)
  NT   Man (Christian theology)
          Woman (Christian theology)
  UF   Anthropology, Biblical
          Bible—Anthropology
          Biblical anthropology
          Theological anthropology (Biblical)

Man and woman (Jewish theology)
  BT   Man and woman (Theology)
  NT   Man (Jewish theology)
          Woman (Jewish theology)
  UF   Anthropology, Biblical
          Bible—Anthropology
          Biblical anthropology
          Theological anthropology (Biblical)

Man and woman (Theology)
  NT   Man (Theology)
          Man and woman (Christian theology)
          Man and woman (Jewish theology)
          Woman (Theology)
  UF   Anthropology, Doctrinal
          Anthropology, Theological
          Doctrinal anthropology
          Theological anthropology

LCSH: Breast—Radiography. LCSH traces a cross reference from Mammography; users, therefore, can get to the material, but Mammography is the term commonly used and provides direct access.

LCSH: Man (Theology)

Manhood (Psychology)
- BT Men—Psychology
      Sex (Psychology)
- RT Androgyny
      Transvestism
- UF Masculine mystique
      Masculinity (Psychology)

Manpower
- USE Human resources

Mariners
- USE Sailors

Marital counseling
- USE Marriage counseling

LC **Marriage**
- RT Extramarital relations
- NT Intermarriage
      Interpersonal relations in marriage
      Marriage (Heterosexual)
      Marriage (Homosexual)
      Marriage alternatives
      Marriage contracts, Extralegal
      Marriage counseling
      Remarriage
      Teen age marriage
- UF Matrimony

LC **Marriage—Annulment**
- RT Divorce
      Divorce and separation counseling
      Separation (Law)
- UF Annulment, Marriage

Marriage—Human relations
- USE Interpersonal relations in marriage

Marriage—Interpersonal relations
- USE Interpersonal relations in marriage

Marriage, Child-free
- USE Child-free marriage

Marriage, Childless
- USE Child-free marriage

Marriage, Common law
- USE Common law marriage

Marriage, Contractual
- USE Contractual marriage

Marriage, Group
- USE Group marriage

Marriage, Interethnic
- USE Interethnic marriage

Marriage, Interfaith
- USE Interreligious marriage

Marriage, Interracial
- USE Interracial marriage

Marriage, Interreligious
- USE Interreligious marriage

Marriage, Mixed
- USE Intermarriage

Marriage, Nonsexist
- USE Interpersonal relations in marriage, Nonsexist

Marriage, Open
- USE Open marriage

LCSH: Masculinity (Psychology).

Marriage, Teen age
  USE   Teen age marriage
Marriage, Transethnic
  USE   Interethnic marriage
Marriage, Transracial
  USE   Interracial marriage
Marriage, Trial
  USE   Unmarried couples
Marriage, Two-step
  USE   Unmarried couples
Marriage (Heterosexual)
  BT   Marriage
  RT   Marriage (Homosexual)
  NT   Homosexuals in heterosexual marriage
  UF   Heterosexual marriage
Marriage (Heterosexual), Homosexual men in
  USE   Homosexual men in heterosexual marriage
Marriage (Heterosexual), Lesbians in
  USE   Lesbians in heterosexual marriage
Marriage (Homosexual)
  BT   Marriage
  RT   Homosexual couples
        Marriage (Heterosexual)
  UF   Homosexual marriage
Marriage alternatives
  BT   Alternative lifestyles
        Marriage
  RT   Family alternatives
  NT   Child-free marriage
        Common law marriage
        Contractual marriage
        Group marriage
        Open marriage
        Swinging and swingers (Sex customs)
        Unmarried couples
Marriage-career conflict, Women's
  USE   Women—Education—Role conflict
        Women—Employment—Role conflict
Marriage contracts, Extralegal
Here are entered works on marriage contracts drawn up by legally married
couples. Works on marriage by contract which is not legally recognized
are entered under CONTRACTUAL MARRIAGE.
  BT   Marriage
  RT   Contractual marriage
  UF   Extralegal marriage contracts
LC **Marriage counseling**
  BT   Counseling
        Marriage
  RT   Divorce counseling
  UF   Counseling, Marital
        Marital counseling
        Marriage guidance
        Premarital counseling
Marriage guidance
  USE   Marriage counseling
Married men
  BT   Married people
        Men
  RT   Househusbands
        Runaway wives, husbands, etc.

Whenever appropriate the subdivisions used under Marriage *should be used under this term and under* Marriage (Homosexual). *The NT's traced under* Marriage *should be expanded, as appropriate, to cover various aspects of this topic and of* Marriage (Homosexual); *e.g.* Interpersonal relations in marriage (Homosexual).

LCSH: Husbands

Married men (cont.)
  UF   Husbands
          Men, Married

Married men—Legal status, laws, etc.
Here are entered works on the effect of marriage on men's legal
responsibilities. General works on legal relations between husband and
wife are entered under HUSBAND AND WIFE.
  BT   Men
  RT   Desertion and nonsupport
          Husband and wife
          Support (Domestic relations)

LC **Married people**
  BT   Marriage
  RT   Husband and wife
  NT   Married men
          Married women

Married women
  BT   Married people
          Women
  RT   Housewives
          ARMY WIVES; CLERGYMEN'S WIVES; PRESIDENTS—UNITED STATES—
             WIVES; WIVES OF TRANSVESTITES; RUNAWAY WIVES, HUSBANDS,
             ETC.; and similar headings
  UF   Wives
          Women, Married

LCSH: Wives. *LCSH uses* Married women *for "works on the legal status of women during marriage, especially on the effect of marriage on their legal capacity." The heading for the above type of material should be* Married women—Legal status, laws, etc. *which is the standard approach to such materials provided in the LCSH. In this list, the LCSH note and all appropriate references have been transferred;* Married women *is the basic heading and is subdivided accordingly.*

Married women—Citizenship
  BT   Married women—Legal status, laws, etc.

Married women—Employment
  RT   Mothers—Employment
  UF   Employment—Married women
          Employment—Wives

LCSH: Wives—Employment.

Married women—Legal status, laws, etc.
Here are entered works on the effect of marriage on women's legal
capacity. General works on legal relations between husband and wife are
entered under HUSBAND AND WIFE. Works on the legal status of women in
general are entered under WOMEN—LEGAL STATUS, LAWS, ETC.
  BT   Women—Legal status, laws, etc.
  RT   Divorced women—Legal status, laws, etc.
          Husband and wife
          Widows—Legal status, laws, etc.
  NT   Married women—Citizenship
          Married woman—Personal name rights

Married women—Personal name rights
  BT   Married women—Legal status, laws, etc.
          Names, Personal—Law
  UF   Women's names (Personal), Change of
          Women's rights to their own name

Marxism and women
  USE   Socialism and women

Marxist feminism
  USE   Feminism, Socialist

Marxist women
  USE   Socialists, Women

Masculine mystique
  USE   Manhood (Psychology)

Masculinity (Psychology)
  USE   Manhood (Psychology)

Mass communication
   USE   Mass media

LC **Mass media**
    NT   Mass media, Nonsexist
          Mass media, Women's
          Sexism in mass media

Mass media, Nonsexist
    BT   Mass media
    RT   Mass media, Women's
          Sexism in mass media
    NT   Advertising, Nonsexist
          Motion pictures, Nonsexist
    UF   Nonsexist mass media

Mass media, Sexism in
   USE   Sexism in mass media

Mass media, Women's
    BT   Mass media
    RT   Mass media, Nonsexist
    NT   Comic books, strips, etc., Women's
          Feminist periodicals
          Feminist publishers and publishing
          Filmmakers, Women
          Women's films
          Women's presses
    UF   Women's mass media

Mastectomy
   USE   Breast cancer—Surgery

Mastectomy counseling and therapy
    BT   Counseling for women
    RT   Breast cancer—Surgery

LC **Masturbation**
    BT   Sexuality
    UF   Autoeroticism

Masturbation (Female)
    BT   Sexuality—Women
    UF   Female masturbation
          Women—Masturbation

Masturbation (Male)
    BT   Sexuality—Men
    UF   Male masturbation
          Men—Masturbation

Maternal deprivation
   USE   Mother-separated children

LC **Maternity leave**
    cf.   note under CHILD CARE LEAVE (MOTHER)
    BT   Leave of absence (Employment)
          Women—Employment
    RT   Child care leave
    NT   Sex discrimination in maternity and child care leave

Maternity leave, Sex discrimination in
   USE   Sex discrimination in maternity and child care leave

LC **Matriarchy**
    RT   Family
          Matrilineal kinship
          Patriarchy

LC **Matrilineal kinship**
    BT   Kinship
    RT   Matriarchy

Matrimony
   USE   Marriage

LC **Medicaid**
    RT   Medicare
    BT   The poor—Medical care—United States
    UF   Medical care assistance programs—United States

Medical and health care
    USE   Medical care

LC **Medical care**
    NT   Sexism in medical care
    UF   Health care
            Health services
            Medical and health care
            Medical services

Medical care, Sexism in
    USE   Sexism in medical care

Medical care assistance programs—United States
    USE   Medicaid
            Medicare

Medical personnel
    UF   Health personnel
            Health sciences personnel
            Medical sciences personnel

Medical personnel—Attitudes
    BT   Attitudes (Psychology)
    NT   Rape—Attitudes of medical personnel

Medical sciences personnel
    USE   Medical personnel

Medical services
    USE   Medical care

Medicare
    BT   Seniors—Medical care—United States
            Social Security
    RT   Medicaid
    UF   Medical care assistance programs—United States

LC **Men**
    NT   Boys
            Criminals, Men
            Fathers
            Homosexual men
            Married men
            Middle aged men
            Prostitutes (Male)
            Senior men
            Single men
            Teen age men
            Working class men

Men—Achievement motivation and sex role
    USE   Achievement motivation and sex role of men

Men—Anatomy
    USE   Human anatomy (Male)

Men—Counseling
    USE   Counseling for men

Men—Crime
    USE   Criminals, Men

Men—Education
    BT   Education
    RT   Education—Curricula, Nonsexist

Men—Education—Nonsexist counseling
    USE   Academic counseling, Nonsexist

Men—Employment
    NT   Child care leave (Father)

NT   College graduate men—Employment
        Employees (Men), Training of
        Occupations, Men's
UF   Employment—Men

Men—Homosexuality
 USE   Homosexuality (Male)

Men—In-service training
 USE   Employees (Men), Training of

Men—Language
 RT   Sexism and language

Men—Masturbation
 USE   Masturbation (Male)

Men—Occupation, Choice of
 USE   Vocational guidance for men

Men—Occupations
 USE   Occupations, Men's

Men—On the job training
 USE   Employees (Men), Training of

Men—Ordination (Christianity)
 USE   Ordination of men (Christianity)

Men—Physiology
 USE   Human physiology (Male)

LC **Men—Psychology**
   BT   Psychology
   NT   Manhood (Psychology)
        Men's liberation
        Rape—Psychological aspects
        Sex role conflict
        Sex role socialization of men
        Woman battering—Psychological aspects

Man—Sex role and achievement motivation
 USE   Achievement motivation and sex role of men

Men—Sex role socialization
 USE   Sex role socialization of men

Men—Sexual behavior
 USE   Sexuality—Men

Men—Sports
 USE   Sports for men

Men—Sterilization
 USE   Sterilization of men (Birth control)

Men—Training on the job
 USE   Employees (Men), Training of

Men—Vocational guidance
 USE   Vocational guidance for men

Men, Counseling for
 USE   Counseling for men

Men, Discrimination against
 USE   Reverse sex discrimination

Men, Divorced
 USE   Divorced men

Men, Ordination of (Christianity)
 USE   Ordination of men (Christianity)

Men, Professional
 USE   Professional men

Men, Senior
 USE   Senior men

Men, Single
 USE   Single men

Men, Teen age
  USE   Teen age men

Men, Unmarried
  USE   Single men

Men and child custody
    BT   Child custody
    NT   Homosexual men and child custody
          Reverse sex discrimination in child custody
    UF   Child custody and men

Men authors
  USE   Authors, Men

Men college graduates
  USE   College graduate men

Men criminals
  USE   Criminals, Men

Men homosexuals
  USE   Homosexual men

Men in business
  USE   Businessmen

Men in children's literature
    RT   Sex role in children's literature
    UF   Children's literature, Men in

Men in the professions
  USE   Professional men

Men offenders
  USE   Criminals, Men

Men prisoners
  USE   Prisoners, Men

Men prostitutes
  USE   Prostitutes (Male)

LC **Menarche**
    BT   Menstruation
    UF   Menstruation, Beginning

LC **Menopause**
    BT   Climacteric
          Middle age women—Health
    RT   Menstruation
          Estrogen replacement therapy
    UF   Change of life in women
          Female cycles
          Women's cycles

Men's attitudes towards women coworkers
  USE   Women—Employment—Attitudes of men

Men's clothing
    BT   Clothing and dress
    RT   Grooming for men

Men's consciousness-raising groups
  USE   Consciousness-raising groups, Men's

Men's grooming
  USE   Grooming for men

Men's jails
  USE   Prisons for men

Men's liberation
    BT   Men—Psychology
          Social movements
    RT   Consciousness-raising groups, Men's
          Sex role conflict
    UF   Men's role liberation

Men's occupations
  USE   Occupations, Men's

Men's prisons
  USE   Prisons for men

Men's role liberation
  USE   Men's liberation

LC **Menstruation**
  RT   Menopause
  NT   Menarche
        Premenstrual tension
  UF   Cycles, Menstrual
        Female cycles
        Periods, Menstrual
        Women—Monthly periods
        Women's cycles

Menstruation, Beginning
  USE   Menarche

Mental health   *LCSH:* Mental hygiene
  RT   Health
  NT   subdivision MENTAL HEALTH under headings for classes of persons;
          e.g. MEN—MENTAL HEALTH; MIDDLE AGE WOMEN—MENTAL
          HEALTH; TEEN AGE WOMEN—MENTAL HEALTH; WOMEN—MENTAL
          HEALTH, etc.
  UF   Hygiene, Mental

Mexican-American women
  BT   Latino women—United States
        Minority women—United States
  UF   Chicanas
        Chicano women

LC **Middle age**
  NT   Middle age men
        Middle age women

Middle age and employment
Here are entered works on middle age as a factor in finding and keeping
suitable employment.
  BT   Age and employment
  UF   Employment and middle age
        Middle age workers

Middle age and employment—Women
  BT   Middle age women—Employment
  RT   Sex discrimination in employment—Middle age women
        Women—Employment reentry

Middle age men
  BT   Men
        Middle age
  UF   Men, Middle age

Middle age women
  BT   Middle age
  BT   Women
  UF   Women, Middle age

Middle age women—Counseling
  USE   Counseling for middle age women

Middle age women—Education
  USE   Women—Adult education

Middle age women—Employment
  NT   Middle age and employment—Women
        Sex discrimination in employment—Middle age women

Middle age women—Employment, Sex discrimination in
  USE   Sex discrimination in employment—Middle age women

Middle age women—Health
- BT   Women—Health
- NT   Menopause

Middle age women—Pregnancy
- BT   Pregnancy
- UF   Change of life pregnancy
- Pregnancy and middle age

Middle age women—Pregnancy—Psychological aspects
- RT   Pregnancy counseling for middle age women

Middle age women—Sex discrimination in employment
- USE   Sex discrimination in employment—Middle age women

Middle age women—Sexuality
- USE   Sexuality—Middle age women

Middle age women—Vocational guidance
- USE   Vocational guidance for women reentering employment

Middle age women, Counseling for
- USE   Counseling for middle age women

Middle age women, Pregnancy counseling for
- USE   Pregnancy counseling for middle age women

Middle age workers
- USE   Middle age and employment

LC **Midwives**
- BT   Obstetrics
- RT   Childbirth at home

Ministers, Women
- USE   Clergywomen

LC **Minorities (Indirect)**
- NT   Minority women
- UF   Ethnic groups

Minorities—Employment (Indirect)
- RT   Discrimination in employment
- NT   Minority women—Employment

Minorities—Employment—United States
- NT   Minority women—Employment—United States

Minority women (Indirect)
- BT   Minorities

Minority women—Education (Indirect)
- BT   Women—Education

Minority women—Education—United States
- NT   AFRICAN-AMERICAN WOMEN—EDUCATION; JEWISH-AMERICAN WOMEN—EDUCATION and similar headings

Minority women—Employment (Indirect)
- BT   Minorities—Employment
- Women—Employment

Minority women—Employment—United States
- BT   Minorities—Employment—United States
- Women—Employment—United States
- NT   African-American women—Employment

Minority women—United States
- BT   Women—United States
- NT   AFRICAN-AMERICAN WOMEN; JEWISH-AMERICAN WOMEN; MEXICAN-AMERICAN WOMEN; LATINO WOMEN—UNITED STATES and similar headings

Miscarriage
- BT   Pregnancy
- RT   Abortion
- UF   Abortion, Spontaneous
- Spontaneous abortion

Miscarriage—Psychological aspects
  RT   Miscarriage counseling
Miscarriage counseling
  BT   Counseling for women
  RT   Miscarriage—Psychological aspects
Misogyny
  RT   Hatred of men
  UF   Hatred of women
Misogyny in literature
  UF   Literature, Misogyny in
Mixed adoption
  USE   Interadoption
Mixed Marriage
  USE   Intermarriage
LC **Monastic and religious life**
  Here are entered general works on monastic and religious life. Works on
  the monastic and religious life of members of specific religions or religious
  denominations are entered under the inverted adjectival form; e.g.
  MONASTIC AND RELIGIOUS LIFE, CATHOLIC.
  RT   Religious life
  NT   Monastic and religious life of men
         Monastic and religious life of women
  UF   Monastic life
         Religious and monastic life

In LCSH this heading is used for both general works and for works on Catholic monastic and religious life

Monastic and religious life of men
  BT   Monastic and religious life
  RT   Monasticism and religious orders for men

LCSH: Monastic and religious life

LC **Monastic and religious life of women**
  BT   Monastic and religious life
  RT   Monasticism and religious orders for women
  UF   Women—Monastic life
         Women—Religious and monastic life
Monastic life
  USE   Monastic and religious life
LC **Monasticism and religious orders**
  Here are entered general works on monasticism and religious orders.
  Works on monasticism and the religious orders of specific religions or
  religious denominations are entered under the inverted adjectival form; e.g.
  MONASTICISM AND RELIGIOUS ORDERS, CATHOLIC.
  NT   Monasticism and religious orders for men
         Monasticism and religious orders for women
  UF   Orders, Monastic
         Religious orders

Monasticism and religious orders for men
  BT   Monasticism and religious orders
  RT   Monastic and religious life of men

LCSH: Monasticism and religious orders

LC **Monasticism and religious orders for women**
  BT   Monasticism and religious orders
  RT   Monastic and religious life of women
  NT   Nuns
  UF   Sisterhoods
Morning-after pill (Birth control)
  USE   Oral contraceptives
Mortgage lending
  USE   Mortgage loans
LC **Mortgage loans**
  NT   Sex discrimination in mortgage loans
  UF   Mortgage lending
         Real estate loans

Mortgage loans, Sex discrimination in
   USE   Sex discrimination in mortgage loans

Mothers, Lesbian
   USE   Lesbian mothers

LC **Mother and child**
    BT   Parent and child
    NT   Mothers and daughters
           Mothers and sons
    UF   Child and mother
           Mother-child relationship
           Child-mother relationship

Mother-child relationship
   USE   Mother and child

Mother-separated children
    BT   Parent-separated children
    RT   Single parent family (Father)
           Single fathers
           Children of divorced parents
    UF   Maternal deprivation
           Deprivation, Maternal
                         LCSH: Maternal deprivation

LC **Mothers**
    BT   Parent and child
           Women
    NT   Lesbian mothers
           Parenting
           Single mothers
           Single parent family (Mother)
           Teen age mothers

LC **Mothers—Employment**
    BT   Women—Employment
    RT   Child care
           Married women—Employment
    UF   Working mothers

Mothers, Single
   USE   Single mothers

Mothers, Teen age
   USE   Teen age mothers

Mothers, Unmarried
   USE   Single mothers

Mothers, Unwed
   USE   Single mothers

LC **Mothers and daughters**
    BT   Mother and child
    UF   Daughters and mothers

LC **Mothers and sons**
    BT   Mother and child
    UF   Sons and mothers

Motion picture distributors, Women's
   USE   Women's film distributors

Motion pictures
    BT   Mass media
    NT   Children's films
           Homosexuals in motion pictures
           Motion pictures, Nonsexist
           Sexism in motion pictures
           Women in motion pictures
           Women's films
    UF   Films
           Movies
           Moving pictures
                         LCSH: Moving pictures

Motion pictures, Feminist
  USE   Feminist films

Motion pictures, Homosexuals in
  USE   Homosexuals in motion pictures

Motion pictures, Lesbians in
  USE   Lesbians in motion pictures

Motion pictures, Nonsexist
  BT   Mass media, Nonsexist
  RT   Sexism in motion pictures
         Women's films
  UF   Nonsexist motion pictures

Motion pictures, Sexism in
  USE   Sexism in motion pictures

Motion pictures, Women in
  USE   Women in motion pictures

Motion pictures, Women's
  USE   Women's films

Motion pictures for children
  USE   Children's films

Movies
  USE   Motion pictures

Moving pictures
  USE   Motion pictures

Moving pictures, Feminist
  USE   Feminist films

Moving pictures, Women's
  USE   Women's films

Moving pictures for children
  USE   Children's films

Multiethnic family
  USE   Interethnic family

Multifaith family
  USE   Interreligious family

Multiracial family
  USE   Interracial family

Mythology, Women in
  USE   Women in folklore and mythology

Name-changing, Personal
  USE   Names, Personal—Law

LC **Names, Personal**
  UF   Forenames
         Personal names
         Surnames

LC **Names, Personal—Law**
  NT   Married women—Personal name rights
         Children, Adopted—Personal name rights
         Divorced people—Personal name rights
  UF   Name-changing, Personal
         Personal names, Change of

National planning
  USE   Economic policy
         Social policy

Natural childbirth
  BT   Childbirth
  RT   Childbirth—Psychological aspects
         Childbirth at home
  NT   Lamaze technique (Obstetrics)
  UF   Childbirth, Natural

In LCSH Lamaze *is a cross reference to* Natural Childbirth *rather than a heading in its own right.*

Navigators
  USE   Sailors

Negroes—United States
  USE   African-Americans; and AFRICAN-AMERICAN WOMEN, AFRICAN-
                AMERICAN GIRLS, etc.

''Nepotism rule'' (Sex discrimination)
Here are entered works on employment practices which prohibit the
employment of husband and wife, or of blood relations, by the same
employer.
  BT   Sex discrimination in employment

Networks of families
  USE   Communal family
             Communally organized groups

Newspapers, Feminist
  USE   Feminist periodicals

Newspapers, Women's
  USE   Periodicals, Women's

No-fault divorce
  USE   Divorce, No-fault

Nonmarital relations
  USE   Extramarital relations

Nonsexist advertising
  USE   Advertising, Nonsexist

Nonsexist children's films
  USE   Children's films, Nonsexist

Nonsexist children's literature
  USE   Children's literature, Nonsexist

Nonsexist counseling
  USE   Counseling, Nonsexist

Nonsexist employment interviewing
  USE   Employment interviewing, Nonsexist

Nonsexist hymns (Christian)
  USE   Hymns (Christian), Nonsexist

Nonsexist interpersonal relations
  USE   Interpersonal relations, Nonsexist

Nonsexist liturgies (Christian)
  USE   Liturgies (Christian), Nonsexist

Nonsexist marriage
  USE   Interpersonal relations in marriage, Nonsexist

Nonsexist mass media
  USE   Mass media, Nonsexist

Nonsexist motion pictures
  USE   Motion pictures, Nonsexist

Nonsexist prayers (Christian)
  USE   Prayers (Christian), Nonsexist

Nonsexist teaching materials
  USE   Teaching materials, Nonsexist

Nonsexist textbooks
  USE   Textbooks, Nonsexist

Nonsexist vocational guidance
  USE   Vocational guidance, Nonsexist

Nonsupport (Domestic relations)
  USE   Desertion and nonsupport

Nuclear family
  USE   Family, Nuclear

Nun authors
  USE   Authors, Nun

LC **Nuns**
Here are entered general works on nuns. Works on nuns of a specific religion are entered under the inverted adjectival form; e.g. NUNS, CATHOLIC.
- BT   Monasticism and religious orders for women
- NT   Nuns, Christian

In LCSH this heading is used for both general works and for works on Catholic nuns.

Nuns—Employment
- BT   Women—Employment

Nuns—Employment in public schools
- BT   Teachers
- UF   Public schools, Nuns employed in

LCSH: Nuns as public school teachers

Nuns, Catholic
- BT   Nuns, Christian
- UF   Catholic nuns
        Catholic sisters
        Sisters, Catholic

Nuns, Christian
- BT   Nuns
- NT   Nuns, Catholic
- UF   Christian nuns
        Christian sisters
        Sisters, Christian

Nuns as authors
- USE   Authors, Nun

Nursemaids
- USE   Child-nurses

LC **Nursery schools**
- RT   Child care centers
        Preschool education

Nursing (Infant feeding)
- USE   Breast feeding

LC **Obstetrics**
- RT   Pregnancy
- NT   Abortion
        Childbirth
        Midwives

Obstetrics—Popular works

Obstetrics—Surgery
- NT   Cesarian section

Occupation, Choice of
- USE   Vocational guidance

LC **Occupational retraining**
- cf.   note under EMPLOYEES, TRAINING OF
- BT   Human resources policy
- RT   Occupational training
        Vocational education
        Vocational guidance
- UF   Job retraining
        Retraining, Occupational
        Retraining, Vocational
        Vocational retraining

Occupational retraining—Feminist perspective
- BT   Human resources policy—Feminist perspective
- RT   Occupational retraining for women
- UF   Feminism and occupational retraining
        Feminism and retraining (Occupational)

Occupational retraining for women
- RT   Vocational guidance for women reentering employment
        Women—Employment reentry

Occupational retraining for women (cont.)
 UF   Women—Occupational retraining
       Women—Retraining, Occupational

LC **Occupational training**
 cf.   note under EMPLOYEES, TRAINING OF
 BT   Human resources policy
 RT   Employees, Training of
       Occupational retraining
       Vocational education
       Vocational guidance
 UF   Job training
       Training, Occupational
       Training, Vocational
       Vocational training

Occupational training—Feminist perspective
 BT   Human resources policy—Feminist perspective

Occupational training for women
 RT   Vocational guidance for women
 UF   Women—Occupational training
       Women—Training, Occupational

Occupations
 RT   Professions
       subdivision VOCATIONAL GUIDANCE under names of occupations
 NT   Occupations, Men's
       Occupations, Women's
       Sex-typing of occupations
 UF   Careers
       Jobs
       Trades

LC **Occupations—Terminology**
 NT   Sexism in occupational terminology (English language)

Occupations, Men's
 BT   Men—Employment
       Occupations
 UF   Men—Occupations
       Men's occupations

Occupations, Sex-typing of
 USE   Sex-typing of occupations

Occupations, Women's
 BT   Occupations
       Women—Employment
 RT   Professional women
 NT   OFFICE WORKERS, WOMEN; PARAPROFESSIONS AND PARAPROFESSIONALS—
             WOMEN and similar headings
 UF   Women—Occupations
       Women's occupations

Occupations, Women's—Status
 NT   OFFICE WORKERS, WOMEN—STATUS and similar headings
 UF   Status of occupations (Women's)
       Status of women's occupations

Offenders, Men
 USE   Criminals, Men

Offenders, Women
 USE   Criminals, Women

LC **Offenses against the person**
 NT   Cruelty to children
       Violence against women
 UF   Crimes against the person
       Person, Crimes against the
       Person, Offenses against the

Office employees
  USE   Office workers

Office workers
  BT   White collar workers
  NT   Clerks
          Receptionists
          Secretaries
          Stenographers
          Typists
  UF   Commercial employees
          Office employees

Office workers, Women
  BT   Occupations, Women's
          Women—Employment
  UF   Women office workers

Office workers, Women—Status
  BT   Occupations, Women's—Status
          Women—Social conditions
  UF   Status of office workers (Women)
          Status of women office workers

Officials
  USE   Public officials

Old age, survivors and disability insurance
  USE   Social security

The old religion, Feminism and
  USE   Feminist wicce and wicceans

Older people
  USE   Seniors

Older workers
  USE   Seniors and employment

On the job training
  USE   Employees, Training of

One-parent adoption
  USE   Single-parent adoption

One-parent family
  USE   Single-parent family

Open housing
  USE   Discrimination in housing

Open marriage
  BT   Marriage alternatives
  UF   Marriage, Open

LC **Oral contraceptives**
  BT   Contraceptives
  UF   Birth control pills
          Contraceptives, Oral
          Morning-after pill (Birth control)
          The pill (Birth control)

Oral contraceptives—Effectiveness

Oral contraceptives—Mental and physiological effects
  UF   Oral contraceptives—Physiological effects
          Oral contraceptives—Psychological aspects

Oral contraceptives—Physiological effects
  USE   Oral contraceptives—Mental and physiological effects

Oral contraceptives—Psychological aspects
  USE   Oral contraceptives—Mental and physiological effects

Orders, Monastic
  USE   Monastic and religious orders

Ordination—Catholic Church
> BT   Ordination (Christianity)
> NT   Ordination of women—Catholic Church

Ordination—Church of England
> BT   Ordination (Christianity)
> NT   Ordination of women—Church of England

Ordination (Christianity)   *LCSH:* Ordination
Here are entered general and comparative works not limited in scope to
one Christian faith or denomination. For works on specific religions and
churches, see ORDINATION—CATHOLIC CHURCH, ORDINATION—CHURCH OF
ENGLAND, etc.
> NT   Ordination—Catholic Church
> Ordination—Church of England
> Ordination of men (Christianity)
> Ordination of women (Christianity)

Ordination (Jewish law)   *LCSH:* Semikhah
> NT   Ordination of women (Jewish law)
> UF   Rabbis—Ordination
> Semikhah

Ordination of men (Christianity)
> BT   Ordination (Christianity)
> UF   Men—Ordination (Christianity)
> Men, Ordination of (Christianity)

Ordination of women—Catholic Church
> BT   Catholic Church and women
> Ordination—Catholic Church
> Ordination of women (Christianity)

Ordination of women—Church of England
> BT   Church of England and women
> Ordination—Church of England
> Ordination of women (Christianity)

Ordination of women (Christianity)
> BT   Clergywomen
> Ordination (Christianity)
> NT   Ordination of women—Catholic Church
> Ordination of women—Church of England
> UF   Women—Ordination (Christianity)
> Women, Ordination of (Christianity)

Ordination of women (Jewish law)
> BT   Ordination (Jewish law)
> Rabbis, Women
> UF   Women—Ordination (Jewish law)
> Women, Ordination of (Jewish law)

LC **Orgasm**
> BT   Sexuality
> NT   Orgasm (Female)
> Orgasm (Male)

Orgasm (Female)
> BT   Orgasm
> Sexuality—Women
> NT   Orgasm, Clitoral
> UF   Female orgasm

Orgasm (Male)
> BT   Orgasm
> Sexuality—Men
> UF   Male orgasm

Orgasm, Clitoral
> BT   Orgasm (Female)
> UF   Clitoral orgasm

Orgies
  USE   Group sex

Overpopulation
  BT   Population
  RT   Population control
  NT   Family planning

Pacificism and feminism
  USE   Feminism and pacificism

Paid housework movement
  USE   Wages for housework movement

Painless labor (Childbirth)
  USE   Lamaze technique (Childbirth)

Paramedics
  BT   Paraprofessions and paraprofessionals
  NT   Paramedics, Women

Paramedics, Women
  BT   Paramedics
  UF   Women paramedics

Paraprofessions and paraprofessionals
Here are entered general works on the paraprofessions and
paraprofessionals. Works on specific paraprofessions are entered under
DENTAL ASSISTANTS, LAW PARAPROFESSIONALS, LIBRARY TECHNICIANS,
PARAMEDICS and similar headings.
  UF   Paraprofessionals

Paraprofessions and paraprofessionals—Women
  BT   Occupations, Women's
          Women—Employment
  UF   Women paraprofessionals

LC **Parent and child**
Here are entered works on the legal responsibilities of parents toward their
minor children and on the relationship between parents and minor
children. Works on the responsibilities of adult children toward their
parents and on the relationship between adult children and their parents
are entered under CHILDREN AND PARENTS.
  RT   Children and parents
          Interpersonal relations
  NT   Boys
          Children of acoholic parents
          Children of divorced parents
          Children of homosexual parents
          Children of older parents
          Children of single parents
          Children of unmarried couples
          Father and child
          Fathers
          Girls
          Homosexual parents
          Mother and child
          Mothers
          Parent-separated children
          Parenting
          Single parent family
  UF   Child and parent
          Parents and children

LC **Parent and child (Law)**
  NT   Adoption
          Child custody
          Child support (Law)
          Desertion and nonsupport

Parent-separated children
- BT Parent and child
- NT Father-separated children
  - Mother-separated children
- UF Parental deprivation
  - Deprivation, Parental

LCSH: Parental deprivation

Parental custody
- USE Child custody

Parental deprivation
- USE Parent-separated children

Parenting
- BT Children—Development and guidance
  - Fathers
  - Mothers
  - Parent and child
- NT Parenting and middle age

Parenting and middle age
- BT Parenting
- RT Children of older parents

Parents, Homosexual
- USE Homosexual parents

Parents and children
- USE Children and parents
  - Parent and child

Parents without partners
- USE Single parent family

LC **Part-time employment**
- RT Job-sharing
- UF Employment, Part-time
  - Part-time work

Part-time employment—Feminist perspective
- BT Human resources policy—Feminist perspective
- RT Women—Part-time employment
- UF Feminism and employment (Part-time)
  - Feminism and part-time employment

Part-time employment—Women
- USE Women—Part-time employment

Part-time work
- USE Part-time employment

Parturition
- USE Childbirth

Paternal deprivation
- USE Father-separated children

Paternity leave
- USE Child care leave (Father)

Patriarchy
- RT Family
  - Matriarchy
  - Patrilineal kinship

In LCSH Patriarchy *is a UF reference to* Family.

Patrilineal kinship
- BT Kinship
- RT Patriarchy

Pauperism
- USE The poor

Pay for housework movement
- USE Wages for housework movement

Peace Movement (1961–1975)
- USE Vietnamese conflict, 1961–1975—Protest movements

Pedagogy
  USE   Education
Penal institutions
  USE   Prisons
           Reformatories
Penitentiaries
  USE   Prisons
LC **Pensions**
  NT   Sex discrimination in pension and social security benefits
  UF   Compensation
           Retirement pensions
People, Single
  USE   Single people
People, Unmarried
  USE   Single people
People's banks
  USE   Credit unions
LC **Periodicals**
  NT   Periodicals, Women's
           Scholarly periodicals
  UF   Magazines
           Serials
Periodicals, Feminist
  USE   Feminist periodicals
Periodicals, Learned
  USE   Scholarly periodicals
Periodicals, Scholarly
  USE   Scholarly periodicals
Periodicals, Women's   *LCSH:* Women's periodicals
  BT   Periodicals
  RT   Sexism in periodicals for women
  NT   Comic books, strips, etc., Women's
           Feminist periodicals
           Scholarly periodicals, Women's
           Women's studies—Periodicals
  UF   Magazines, Women's
           Women's magazines
           Women's newspapers
           Women's periodicals
Periodicals, Women's (Sexism in)
  USE   Sexism in periodicals for women
Periods, Menstrual
  USE   Menstruation
Person, Crimes against the
  USE   Offenses against the person
Person, Offenses against the
  USE   Offenses against the person
Personal names
  USE   Names, Personal
Personal names, Change of
  USE   Names, Personal—Law
Personal security for women
  NT   Self-defense for women
  UF   Security, Personal (Women)
           Women—Personal security
           Women—Security, Personal
           Women, Personal security for
LC **Physical education and training**
  BT   Education

Physical education and training (cont.)
   NT   PHYSICAL EDUCATION FOR CHILDREN; PHYSICAL EDUCATION FOR MEN;
              PHYSICAL EDUCATION FOR WOMEN; etc.
   UF   Education, Physical

Physicians, Women
   BT   Professional women
   UF   Women physicians

Physiology, Female (Human)
   USE   Human physiology (Female)

Physiology, Human
   USE   Human physiology

Physiology, Male (Human)
   USE   Human physiology (Male)

The pill (Birth control)
   USE   Oral contraceptives

Pioneer life
   USE   Frontier and pioneer life

Pioneer women
   RT   Frontier and pioneer life of women
   UF   Women pioneers

LC **Pioneers**
   RT   Frontier and pioneer life
   NT   Pioneer women

Placenta previa
   USE   Childbirth—Labor, Complicated

Planned parenthood
   USE   Family planning

Planning, Economic
   USE   Economic policy

Planning, National
   USE   Economic policy
           Social policy

Planning, State
   USE   Economic policy
           Social policy

Poetry, Feminist
   USE   Feminist poetry

Police—Attitudes
   BT   Attitudes (Psychology)
   NT   Rape—Attitudes of police

Political activism—Women
   RT   Politicians, Women
           Politics, Practical—Women's activism
   UF   Women—Political activism
           Women and politics
           Women in politics

LCSH: Women in politics. *The LCSH heading is assigned by LC to works on women who are active in politics and to works on professional women politicians.*

Politicians (Indirect)
   BT   World leaders
   NT   Politicians, Women

LCSH: Statesmen. *Which is something of an overstatement.*

Politicians—United States
   NT   Legislators—United States

Politicians, Women
   RT   Political activism—Women
           Politics, Practical—Women's activism
           Public officers, Women
   NT   Legislators, Women
   UF   Women—Political activism
           Women and politics
           Women in politics
           Women politicians

LCSH: Women in politics

Politics, Feminist
USE   Feminist politics

LC **Politics, Practical**
NT   Women's movement (1960–   ) and practical politics
UF   Practical politics

Politics, Practical—Women's activism
RT   Political activism—Women
       Politicians, Women
NT   Women's movement (1960–   ) and practical politics
UF   Women—Political activism
       Women and politics
       Women in politics

LC **Polyandry**
BT   Polygamy

LC **Polygamy**
NT   Group marriage
       Polyandry
       Polygyny

The LCSH heading is used for works on marriage between plural husbands and plural wives and for works specifically on plural wives.

Polygyny
BT   Polygamy

The poor (Indirect)
NT   Poor women
UF   Economically disadvantaged
       Pauperism

LCSH: Poor

The poor—Medical care (Indirect)

The poor—Medical care—United States
NT   Medicaid

Poor women (Indirect)
BT   The poor
       Women—Economic conditions
RT   Senior women—Economic conditions
UF   Women, Poor

LC **Population**
NT   Overpopulation
       Population control

Population control
BT   Population
RT   Overpopulation
NT   Family planning
UF   Fertility limitation, Human
       Human fertility limitation

Post graduate work
USE   Higher education—Graduate work

Practical politics
USE   Politics, Practical

Prayers (Christian), Nonsexist
UF   Nonsexist prayers (Christian)

Emswiler, Sharon Neufer. Women and worship; a guide to non-sexist hymns, prayers, and liturgies *(1974)*

LC **Pregnancy**
RT   Obstetrics
NT   Abortion
       Childbirth
       Middle age women—Pregnancy
       Miscarriage
       Single women—Pregnancy
       Teen age women—Pregnancy
UF   Child-bearing
       Gestation

LC **Pregnancy—Psychological aspects**
RT   Abortion—Psychological aspects
       Pregnancy counseling

Pregnancy and middle age
USE   Middle age women—Pregnancy

Pregnancy and teen age
USE   Teen age women—Pregnancy

Pregnancy counseling
BT   Counseling for women
RT   Abortion counseling
         Pregnancy—Psychological aspects
NT   Pregnancy counseling for middle age women
         Pregnancy counseling for single women
         Pregnancy counseling for teen age women

Pregnancy counseling for middle age women
BT   Counseling for middle age women
         Pregnancy counseling
RT   Middle age women—Pregnancy—Psychological aspects
UF   Middle age women, Pregnancy counseling for

Pregnancy counseling for single women
BT   Pregnancy counseling
RT   Single women—Pregnancy—Psychological aspects
UF   Single women, Pregnancy counseling for

Pregnancy counseling for teen age women
BT   Counseling for teen age women
         Pregnancy counseling
RT   Teen age women—Pregnancy—Psychological aspects
UF   Teen age women, Pregnancy counseling for

Pregnant teen agers
USE   Teen age women—Pregnancy

Premarital counseling
USE   Marriage counseling

Premarital relations
USE   Extramarital relations

Premature labor (Childbirth)
USE   Childbirth—Labor, Premature

Premenstrual tension
BT   Menstruation
UF   Premenstruation (Cyclical phenomenon)
         Tension, Premenstrual

Premenstruation (Cyclical phenomenon)
USE   Premenstrual tension

LCSH: Premenstrual syndrome. In Woman, dependent or independent variable? (1975), the term "cyclical phenomenon" is preferred to premenstrual "syndrome" since the former term emphasizes the physiological nature of premenstrual changes such as cramps, mood swings, backache, and depression while the latter term implies that these changes are pathological. It was generally agreed, however, that Cyclical phenomenon (Premenstruation) would not serve users. The neutral Premenstrual tension is recommended.

LCSH: Education, Preschool

Preschool education
BT   Education
RT   Child care centers
         Nursery schools
UF   Education, Preschool
         Infant school

Priests, Women
USE   Clergywomen (Christianity)

Primary education
BT   Education
UF   Education, Primary
         Grade school education

LCSH: Education, Primary

Primary education—Curricula

Primary education—Curricula, Nonsexist
   RT   Girls—Education
           Sexism in curricula (Primary education)
   UF   Primary education—Nonsexist curricula

Primary education—Nonsexist curricula
   USE Primary education—Curricula, Nonsexist

Primary education—Sexism in curricula
   USE Sexism in curricula (Primary education)

LC **Prisoners**
   RT   Crime and criminals
           Prisons
   NT   Prisoners, Men
           Prisoners, Women
   UF   Convicts

Prisoners, Men
   BT   Prisoners
   RT   Criminals, Men
           Prisons for men
   UF   Men prisoners

Prisoners, Women
   BT   Prisoners
   RT   Criminals, Women
           Prisons for women
   UF   Women prisoners

LC **Prisons**
   RT   Reformatories
   NT   Prisons for men
           Prisons for women
   UF   Jails
           Penal institutions
           Penitentiaries

Prisons for men
   BT   Prisons
   RT   Criminals, Men
           Prisoners, Men
           Reformatories for boys
   UF   Men's jails
           Men's prisons

Prisons for women
   BT   Prisons
   RT   Criminals, Women
           Prisoners, Women
           Reformatories for girls
   UF   Women's jails
           Women's prisons

LCSH: Reformatories for women

Private household workers
   USE Household workers

Pro-life movement
   USE Right to life movement

Professional associations
   USE Trade and professional associations

Professional men
   BT   Professions
   UF   Men, Professional
           Men in the professions

Professional unions
   RT   Labor unions
   NT   Librarians' unions
   UF   Unions, Professional

Professional women
- BT   Profession
-        Women—Employment
- RT   Occupations, Women's
- NT   COUNSELORS, WOMEN; LIBRARIANS, WOMEN; PHYSICIANS, WOMEN; and
-        similar headings
- UF   Women, Professional
-        Women in the professions

Professional women—Status
- BT   Women—Social conditions
- NT   COUNSELORS, WOMEN—STATUS and similar headings
- UF   Status of women in the professions

LC **Professions**
- RT   Occupations
-        subdivision VOCATIONAL GUIDANCE under name of professions
- NT   Professional men
-        Professional women
- UF   Careers
-        Jobs

Professions, Choice of
- USE   Vocational guidance

Programs, Radio (Sexism in)
- USE   Sexism in radio programs

Programs, Television (Sexism in)
- USE   Sexism in television programs

Progressivism (United States politics) and feminism
- USE   Feminism and Progressivism (United States politics)

Prophylactic (Birth control device)
- USE   Condoms

Prostitutes
- BT   Prostitution
- NT   Prostitutes (Child)
-        Prostitutes(Female)
-        Prostitutes (Male)
- UF   Hookers
-        Streetwalkers

Prostitutes—Legal status, laws, etc.
- RT   Prostitution—Law and legislation

Prostitutes (Child)
- BT   Juvenile delinquents
-        Prostitutes
- UF   Child prostitutes

Prostitutes (Female)
- BT   Prostitutes
-        Women
- UF   Female prostitutes
-        Women prostitutes

Prostitutes (Female)—Legal status, laws, etc.
- BT   Women—Legal status, laws, etc.
- NT   Prostitutes' Decriminalization Movement

Prostitutes (Male)
- BT   Men
-        Prostitutes
- UF   Male prostitutes
-        Men prostitutes

Prostitutes' Decriminalization Movement
- BT   Prostitutes (Female)—Legal status, laws, etc.
- RT   Prostitution—Law and legislation, Discriminatory
- UF   Decriminalization Movement, Prostitutes'

LC **Prostitution**
 RT Extramarital relations
 NT Prostitutes

Prostitution—Discriminatory law and legislation
 USE Prostitution—Law and legislation, Discriminatory

Prostitution—Law and legislation
 BT Sex and law
 RT Prostitutes—Legal status, laws, etc.

Prostitution—Law and legislation, Discriminatory
 BT Women—Legal status, laws, etc.—Discriminatory legislation
 RT Prostitutes' Decriminalization Movement
 UF Prostitution—Discriminatory law and legislation

Protective law and legislation (Women)
 USE Women—Legal status, laws, etc.—Discriminatory legislation

Protest movements, Anti-war (1961–1975)
 USE Vietnamese conflict, 1961–1975—Protest movements

LC **Psychoanalysis**
 NT Feminist psychoanalysis
   Sexism in psychoanalysis

Psychoanalysis, Feminist
 USE Feminist psychoanalysis

Psychoanalysis, Sexism in
 USE Sexism in psychoanalysis

Psychological counseling and therapy referral services, Feminist
 USE Feminist psychological counseling and therapy referral services

LC **Psychology**
 NT Aggressiveness (Psychology)
   Assertiveness (Psychology)
   Feminist psychology
   Men—Psychology
   Sexism in psychology
   Women—Psychology

Psychology, Feminist
 USE Feminist psychology

Psychology, Sexism in
 USE Sexism in psychology

Psychology, Sexual
 USE Sex (Psychology)

Psychology of sex
 USE Sex (Psychology)

Psychoprophylactic childbirth
 USE Lamaze technique (Childbirth)

LC **Psychotherapy**
 NT Feminist psychotherapy
   Sexism in psychotherapy

Psychotherapy, Feminist
 USE Feminist psychotherapy

Psychotherapy, Sexism in
 USE Sexism in psychotherapy

Public accommodations, Discrimination in
 USE Discrimination in public accommodations

Public accommodations, Sex discrimination in
 USE Sex discrimination in public accommodations

Public officers
 USE Public officials

Public officials   *LCSH:* Public officers
 NT Local officials and employees
   State governments—Officials and employees

Public officials (cont.)
UF   Government officials
       Officials
       Public officers

Public officials, Women   *LCSH:* Women in public life
RT   Politicians, Women
UF   Women government officials
       Women public officers

Public policy
USE   Economic policy
        Social policy

Public schools, Nuns employed in
USE   Nuns—Employment in public schools

LC **Publishers and publishing**
NT   Feminist publishers and publishing
       Small presses
       Women's presses
UF   Book trade

Publishers and publishing, Feminist
USE   Feminist publishers and publishing

Publishers and publishing, Small press
USE   Small presses

Publishers and publishing, Women
USE   Women's presses

Puerto Rican-American women
BT   Latino women—United States

LC **Rabbis**
NT   Rabbis, Women
UF   Jewish rabbis

Rabbis—Ordination
USE   Ordination (Jewish law)

Rabbis, Women
RT   Clergywomen (Christianity)
NT   Ordination of women (Jewish law)
UF   Women rabbis

Racial interadoption
USE   Interracial adoption

Racial intermarriage
USE   Interracial marriage

Radical feminism
USE   Feminism, Radical

Radical mastectomy
USE   Breast cancer—Surgery

Radio programs, Sexism in
USE   Sexism in radio programs

LC **Rape**
BT   Violence against women
RT   Anti-rape movements
UF   Assault, Criminal (Against women)
       Criminal assault against women

Rape—Attitudes of medical personnel
BT   Medical personnel—Attitudes
       Rape—Psychological aspects
       Sexism in medical care
UF   Rape—Medical personnel's attitudes

Rape—Attitudes of police
BT   Police—Attitudes
       Rape—Psychological aspects
UF   Rape—Police attitudes

Rape—Law and legislation

Rape—Law and legislation, Discriminatory
    BT   Women—Legal status, laws, etc.—Discriminatory legislation
    RT   Anti-rape movements
    UF   Rape—Discriminatory law and legislation

Rape—Law reform movement
    USE   Anti-rape movements

Rape—Medical personnel's attitudes
    USE   Rape—Attitudes of medical personnel

Rape—Police attitude
    USE   Rape—Attitudes of police

Rape—Psychological aspects
    BT   Men—Psychology
           Women—Psychology
    RT   Rape crisis centers
    NT   Rape—Attitudes of medical personnel
           Rape—Attitudes of police

Rape—Self-help and law reform
    USE   Anti-rape movements

Rape crisis centers
    BT   Women's projects and services
    RT   Anti-rape movements
           Rape—Psychological aspects

Real estate loans
    USE   Mortgage loans

LC **Receptionists**
    BT   Office workers
    RT   Secretaries

Receptionists, Women
    UF   Women receptionists (Office workers)

Reentry into employment, Women's
    USE   Women—Employment reentry

Reform schools
    USE   Reformatories

LC **Reformatories**
    RT   Juvenile delinquency
           Juvenile detention homes
           Prisons
    NT   Reformatories (Female)
           Reformatories (Male)
    UF   Penal institutions
           Reform schools
           Remand homes

Reformatories (Female)
    BT   Reformatories
    UF   Girls' reformatories

Reformatories (Male)
    BT   Reformatories
    UF   Boys' reformatories

Refuges, Women's
    USE   Women's shelters

Religion and sex
    USE   Sex and religion

Religion and women
Here are entered works on the status of women in religious traditions. For works on the theological position of women in religion see WOMAN (THEOLOGY). For works on the day-to-day religious practices of women see RELIGIOUS LIFE—WOMEN.
    RT   Religious life—Women
           Women (Theology)

Religion and women (cont.)
   NT   Christianity and women
           Judaism and women
   UF   Women and religion
           Women in religion

Religious and monastic life
  USE   Monastic and religious life

Religious interadoption
  USE   Interreligious adoption

Religious intermarriage
  USE   Interreligious marriage

Religious life
Here are entered works on day-to-day religious practices of lay persons.
Works on the religious life of non-lay persons are entered under MONASTIC
AND RELIGIOUS LIFE.
   RT   Monastic and religious life

Religious life—Women
   RT   Religion and women; cf. note under RELIGION AND WOMEN
   UF   Women—Religious life
           Women and religion

Religious life (Christianity)
   UF   Christian life
           Discipleship (Christianity)

Religious life (Christianity)—Women
   RT   Christianity and women; cf. note under CHRISTIANITY AND WOMEN

Religious life (Judaism)
   BT   Jews—Social life and customs
   UF   Jewish life (Religious)

Religious life (Judaism)—Women
   RT   Judaism and women; cf. note under JUDAISM AND WOMEN

Religious orders
  USE   Monastic and religious orders

Remand homes
  USE   Juvenile detention homes
          Reformatories

LC **Remarriage**
   BT   Divorced people
           Marriage
           Widowers
           Widows

Retail clerks
  USE   Clerks (Retail trade)

Retirement pensions
  USE   Pensions

Retraining, Occupational
  USE   Occupational retraining

Retraining, Vocational
  USE   Occupational retraining

Reverse sex discrimination
Here are entered general works on sex based discrimination against men.
Works on sex based discrimination against women are entered under SEX
DISCRIMINATION.
   BT   Discrimination
   NT   Reverse sex discrimination in child care leave
           Reverse sex discrimination in child custody
   UF   Discrimination against men
           Discrimination, Sex
           Men, Discrimination against
           Sex discrimination against men

LCSH: Christian life. *The change is recommended simply for the sake of consistency; comparable headings for other religions are constructed in LCSH as* Religious life (Buddhism), Religious life (Islam), *etc.*

LCSH: Jewish way of life. *This change is recommended both for purposes of consistency in the approach to material and because it was generally agreed that* Jewish way of life *was much broader than Jewish religious life. The use of* Jews—Social life and customs *is recommended for general works on Jewish customs and traditions.*

Reverse sex discrimination in child care leave
    BT   Child care leave (Father)
            Reverse sex discrimination
    UF   Paternity leave
            Sex discrimination in child care leave

Reverse sex discrimination in child custody
    BT   Men and child custody
            Reverse sex discrimination
    UF   Sex discrimination in child custody, Reverse

Reversing roles
    USE   Role reversal

LC **Rhythym method (Birth control)**
    BT   Birth control
    UF   Safe period intercourse (Birth control)

Rhythm method (Birth control)—Effectiveness
    BT   Birth control—Effectiveness

Right to life movement
    RT   Abortion—Law and legislation
    UF   Pro-life movement

Rights, Civil
    USE   Civil rights

Rights of women
    USE   Women—Civil rights

LC **Role conflict**
    RT   Role reversal
    NT   Sex role conflict

Role models
    BT   Social role
    RT   Role reversal

Role reversal
    BT   Sex role
            Social role
    RT   Role conflict
            Role models
    UF   Reversing roles
            Role switching
            Switching roles

Role switching
    USE   Role reversal

"Rubbers" (Birth control device)
    USE   Condoms

Runaway husbands
    USE   Runaway wives, husbands, etc.

Runaway wives, husbands, etc.
Here are entered general works on people who *run away* from
interpersonal responsibilities. Works on the legal responsibility of
husbands to support their families are entered under DESERTION AND
NONSUPPORT and SUPPORT (DOMESTIC RELATIONS)
    RT   Desertion and nonsupport
            Married men
            Married women
            Support (Domestic relations)
    UF   Husbands, Runaway
            Runaway husbands
            Wives, Runaway

Safe period intercourse (Birth control)
    USE   Rhythm method (Birth control)

Sailors   *LCSH:* Seamen
    UF   Life at sea
            Mariners

Sailors (cont.)
UF   Navigators
       Seafarers
       Seamen

Sailors, Women [African-American, Jewish, etc.]
UF   Women [African-American, Jewish, etc.] sailors

LCSH: Women and the sea, Jews as seamen, Negroes as seamen

Sales men
USE   Salesmen

LC **Sales personnel**
BT   White collar workers
RT   Clerks (Retail trade)
NT   Salesmen
       Saleswomen
UF   Salespeople

Sales women
USE   Saleswomen

Salesclerks
USE   Clerks (Retail trade)

Salesmen
BT   Sales personnel
UF   Sales men

Saleswomen
BT   Sales personnel
UF   Sales women

Same-sex lifestyle
USE   Homosexuality
       Homosexuals

LC **Scholarly periodicals**
BT   Periodicals
NT   Scholarly periodicals, Women's
UF   Learned periodicals
       Periodicals, Learned
       Periodicals, Scholarly

Scholarly periodicals, Women's
BT   Periodicals, Women's
       Scholarly periodicals
UF   Women's learned periodicals
       Women's scholarly periodicals

School books
USE   Textbooks

School life
USE   Student life and customs

Schools—Curricula
USE   Education—Curricula

Seafarers
USE   Sailors

Seamen
USE   Sailors

Secondary education
BT   Education
UF   Education, Secondary
       High school education

LCSH: Education, Secondary

Secondary education—Curricula

Secondary education—Curricula, Nonsexist
RT   Sexism in curricula (Secondary education)
       Teen age women—Education
UF   Secondary education—Nonsexist curricula

Secondary education—Nonsexist curricula
USE   Secondary education—Curricula, Nonsexist

Secondary education—Sexism in curricula
  USE   Sexism in curricula (Secondary education)

Secretaries
  BT   Office workers
  RT   Receptionists

Secretaries, Women
  UF   Women secretaries

Security, Personal (Women)
  USE   Personal security for women

Segregation in housing
  USE   Discrimination in housing

Segregation in public accommodations
  USE   Discrimination in public accommodations

LC **Self-defense for women**
  BT   Anti-rape movements
         Personal security for women
  UF   Women—Defense
         Women—Self defense

Semen banks
  USE   Sperm banks

Semikhah
  USE   Ordination (Jewish law)

Senators (United States), Women
  BT   Legislators, Women—United States
  UF   Congresswomen (Senate)
         Women senators (United States)

Senior citizens
  USE   Seniors

Senior men
  BT   Men
         Seniors
  UF   Men, Senior

Senior women
  BT   Women
         Seniors
  UF   Women, Senior

Senior women—Counseling
  USE   Counseling for senior women

Senior women—Economic conditions
  RT   Poor women

Senior women—Education
  USE   Women—Adult education

Senior women—Employment
  NT   Seniors and employment—Women
         Sex discrimination in employment—Senior women

Senior women—Employment, Sex discrimination in
  USE   Sex discrimination in employment—Senior women

Senior women—Sex discrimination in employment
  USE   Sex discrimination in employment—Senior women

Senior women—Sexuality
  USE   Sexuality—Senior women

Senior women—Vocational guidance
  USE   Vocational guidance for women reentering employment

Senior women, Counseling for
  USE   Counseling for senior women

Seniors
  NT   Senior men
         Senior women
  UF   The aged
         Elderly persons

Seniors (cont.)
UF   Older people
      Senior citizens

Seniors—Alternative lifestyles
BT   Alternative lifestyles
      Seniors—Personal conduct, lifestyles, etc.

Seniors—Medical care—United States
NT   Medicare

Seniors—Personal conduct, lifestyles, etc.
NT   Seniors—Alternative lifestyles

Seniors and employment
Here are entered works on aging as a factor in finding and keeping suitable employment.
BT   Age and employment
UF   Elderly workers
      Employment and seniors
      Older workers

Seniors and employment—Women
BT   Senior women—Employment
RT   Sex discrimination in employment—Senior women
      Women—Employment reentry

LC **Separation (Law)**
RT   Divorce
      Divorce and separation counseling
      Husband and wife
      Marriage—Annulment
NT   Separation (Marital relations)

Separation (Marital relations)
Here are entered works on legally married couples who mutually consent to separate without changing their legal status as husband and wife.
BT   Separation (Law)

Separation and divorce counseling
USE   Divorce and separation counseling

Serials
USE   Periodicals

Servants
USE   Household workers

LC **Sex (Psychology)**
RT   Sex counseling and therapy
NT   Manhood (Psychology)
      Sex role
      Sexuality
      Womanhood (Psychology)
UF   Gender identity
      Psychology, Sexual
      Psychology of sex
      Sexual psychology

Sex, Extramarital
USE   Extramarital relations

Sex and Christianity
BT   Sex and religion
UF   Christianity and sex

LC **Sex and law**
NT   Abortion—Law and legislation
      Artificial insemination, Human—Law and legislation
      Birth control—Law and legislation
      Homosexuality—Law and legislation
      Prostitution—Law and legislation
UF   Law and sex

LC **Sex and religion**
NT   Sex and Christianity
UF   Religion and sex

LCSH: Aged—Conduct of life

Sex change
　USE　Transsexual surgery

Sex counseling and therapy
　BT　Counseling
　　　Sexuality
　RT　Sex (Psychology)
　UF　Sex therapy
　　　Sexual counseling and therapy
　　　Sexual therapy

LC **Sex customs**
　NT　Sexual freedom

LC **Sex differences**
　RT　Androgyny

Sex discrimination
Here are entered general works on sex based discrimination against
women. Works on sex based discrimination against men are entered under
REVERSE SEX DISCRIMINATION.
　BT　Discrimination
　　　Women—Civil rights
　RT　Feminism
　NT　headings beginning with the words SEX DISCRIMINATION
　UF　Discrimination against women
　　　Discrimination, Sex
　　　Sexual discrimination
　　　Women, Discrimination against

LCSH: Sex discrimination against
women

Sex discrimination—Economic aspects
　RT　Economic policy—Feminist perspective
　NT　Sex discrimination in consumer credit
　　　Sex discrimination in mortgage loans

LC **Sex discrimination—Law and legislation**
　BT　Women—Legal status, laws, etc.
　NT　Sex discrimination in employment—Law and legislation

Sex discrimination against men
　USE　Reverse sex discrimination

Sex discrimination in child care leave
　USE　Reverse sex discrimination in child care leave
　　　Sex discrimination in maternity and child care leave

Sex discrimination in child custody, Reverse
　USE　Reverse sex discrimination in child custody

Sex discrimination in consumer credit
　BT　Consumer credit
　　　Sex discrimination—Economic aspects
　RT　Feminist credit unions
　　　Sex discrimination in mortgage loans
　UF　Consumer credit, Sex discrimination in

LC **Sex discrimination in education**
　BT　Discrimination in education
　NT　Sexism in academic counseling
　　　Sexism in curricula
　　　Sexism in educational tests and measurements
　　　Sexism in vocational guidance
　UF　Education, Sex discrimination in

Sex discrimination in employment
　BT　Discrimination in employment
　　　Women—Employment
　RT　Age discrimination in employment
　　　Sexism in employment
　　　Women—Employment—Attitudes of employers
　NT　Equal pay for equal work—Women workers
　　　"Nepotism rule" (Sex discrimination)
　　　Sex discrimination in government employment
　　　Sex discrimination in maternity and child care leave

Sex discrimination in employment (cont.)
- NT   Sex discrimination in labor unions
  - Sex discrimination in pensions and social security benefits
  - Sex discrimination in wages
  - BUSINESSWOMEN—STATUS; ATHLETICS COACHES, WOMEN—STATUS; COUNSELORS, WOMEN—STATUS and similar headings under names of professions and occupations.

Sex discrimination in employment—Law and legislation
- BT   Labor laws and legislation—Women
  - Sex discrimination—Law and legislation
- RT   Affirmative action for women

Sex discrimination in employment—Middle age women
- BT   Middle age women—Employment
- RT   Middle age and employment—Women
- UF   Middle age women—Employment, Sex discrimination in
  - Middle age women—Sex discrimination in employment

Sex discrimination in employment—Senior women
- BT   Senior women—Employment
- RT   Seniors and employment—Women
- UF   Senior women—Sex discrimination in employment

Sex discrimination in employment—Teen age women
- BT   Teen age women—Employment
- RT   Teen age and employment—Women
- UF   Teen age women—Employment, Sex discrimination in
  - Teen age women—Sex discrimination in employment

Sex discrimination in government employment
- BT   Sex discrimination in employment
- UF   Civil service, Sex discrimination in
  - Government employment, Sex discrimination in

Sex discrimination in housing
- BT   Discrimination in housing
- RT   Sex discrimination in mortgage loans
- UF   Housing, Sex discrimination in

Sex discrimination in labor laws and legislation
- USE   Labor laws and legislation, Discriminatory—Women

Sex discrimination in labor unions
- BT   Sex discrimination in employment
- RT   Labor unionists, Women
  - Sexism in labor unions
- UF   Labor unions, Sex discrimination in
  - Sex discrimination in trade unions

Sex discrimination in law and legislation
- USE   Women—Legal status, laws, etc.—Discriminatory legislation

Sex discrimination in maternity and child care leave
- BT   Child care leave (Mother)
  - Maternity leave
  - Sex discrimination in employment
- UF   Child care leave (Mother), Sex discrimination in
  - Maternity leave, Sex discrimination in
  - Sex discrimination in child care leave

Sex discrimination in mortgage loans
- BT   Mortgage loans
  - Sex discrimination—Economic aspects
- RT   Feminist credit unions
  - Sex discrimination in consumer credit
  - Sex discrimination in housing
- UF   Mortgage loans, Sex discrimination in

Sex discrimination in pensions and social security benefits
- BT   Sex discrimination in employment
  - Pensions
  - Social security

UF   Sex discrimination in retirement benefits
        Sex discrimination in social security benefits

Sex discrimination in public accommodations
   BT   Discrimination in public accommodations
   UF   Public accommodations, Sex discrimination in

Sex discrimination in retirement benefits
   USE   Sex discrimination in pensions and social security benefits

Sex discrimination in social security benefits
   USE   Sex discrimination in pensions and social security benefits

Sex discrimination in trade unions
   USE   Sex discrimination in labor unions

Sex discrimination in wages
   BT   Sex discrimination in employment
        Wages—Women
   RT   Equal pay for equal work—Women workers
   UF   Wages, Sex discrimination in

LC **Sex role**
   BT   Sex (Psychology)
   RT   Social role
   NT   Androgyny
        Role reversal
        Sex role conflict
        Sex role socialization
        Transvestism
        Transsexuality
   UF   Gender identity

Sex role and achievement motivation
   USE   Achievement motivation and sex role

Sex role conflict
   BT   Men—Psychology
        Role conflict
        Sex role
        Women—Psychology
   RT   Achievement motivation and sex role
        Men's liberation
   NT   WOMEN—EDUCATION, HIGHER—ROLE CONFLICT; WOMEN—
          EMPLOYMENT—ROLE CONFLICT and similar headings

Sex role in children's literature
   BT   Sex role in literature
        Sex role socialization
   RT   Men in children's literature
        Sex role socialization of children
        Women in children's literature
   NT   Children's literature, Nonsexist
        Sexism in children's literature
   UF   Children's literature, Sex role in

Sex role in literature
   BT   Women in literature
   RT   Literature—History and criticism—Feminist perspective
   NT   Sex role in children's literature
   UF   Literature, Sex role in

Sex role in literature (American)
   RT   American literature—History and criticism—Feminist perspective
   UF   American literature, Sex role in

Sex role in literature (English)
   RT   English literature—History and criticism—Feminist perspective
   UF   English literature, Sex role in

Sex role inversion
   USE   Transsexuality

Sex role socialization
   BT   Sex role
        Socialization

Sex role socialization (cont.)
   NT   Sex role socialization of children
           Sex role socialization of men
           Sex role socialization of women
           Sexism in children's literature
           Sexism in mass media
           Sexism in textbooks

Sex role socialization of boys
   USE   Sex role socialization of children

Sex role socialization of children
   BT   Sex role socialization
   RT   Sex role socialization of men
           Sex role socialization of women
   NT   Sexism in children's literature
           Sexism in textbooks (Primary education)
           Sexism in textbooks (Secondary education)
   UF   Boys—Sex role socialization
           Children—Sex role socialization
           Girls—Sex role socialization
           Sex role socialization of boys
           Sex role socialization of girls

Sex role socialization of girls
   USE   Sex role socialization of children

Sex role socialization of men
   BT   Men—Psychology
           Sex role socialization
   RT   Sex role socialization of children
   NT   Sexism in textbooks (Higher education)
           Sexism in textbooks (Secondary education)
   UF   Men—Sex role socialization
           Sex role socialization of teen age men
           Teen age men—Sex role socialization

Sex role socialization of teen age men
   USE   Sex role socialization of men

Sex role socialization of teen age women
   USE   Sex role socialization of women

Sex role socialization of women
   BT   Sex role socialization
           Women—Psychology
   RT   Aggressiveness (Psychology) in women
           Assertiveness (Psychology) in women
           Sex role socialization of children
           Sexism in textbooks (Higher education)
           Sexism in textbooks (Secondary education)
   UF   Sex role socialization of teen age women
           Teen age women—Sex role socialization
           Women—Sex role socialization

Sex therapy
   USE   Sex counseling and therapy

Sex-typing of occupations
   BT   Discrimination in employment
           Occupations
   RT   Feminist vocational guidance
           Sexism in vocational guidance
           Vocational guidance, Nonsexist
           Vocational guidance for men
           Vocational guidance for women
   UF   Occupations, Sex-typing of
           Stereotyping of occupations

Sexism in academic counseling
   BT   Sex discrimination in education
   RT   Academic counseling, Nonsexist

    RT   Women—Education—Role conflict
    UF   Women—Education—Sexism in counseling

Sexism in advertising
    BT   Sexism in mass media
    RT   Advertising, Nonsexist
    UF   Advertising, Sexism in

Sexism in children's literature
    BT   Sex role in children's literature
            Sex role socialization of children
    RT   Children's literature, Nonsexist
    NT   Sexism in textbooks (Primary education)
            Sexism in textbooks (Secondary education)
    UF   Children's literature, Sexism in

Sexism in counseling
    BT   Counseling
    RT   Counseling, Nonsexist
            Counseling for men
            Counseling for women
            Feminist counseling and therapy
    UF   Counseling, Sexism in

Sexism in curricula
    BT   Sex discrimination in education
    RT   Education—Curricula, Nonsexist
    UF   Education—Sexism in curricula

Sexism in curricula (Higher education)
    RT   Higher education—Curricula, Nonsexist
    NT   Sexism in textbooks (Higher education)
    UF   Higher education—Sexism in curricula
            Universities and colleges—Sexism in curricula

Sexism in curricula (Primary education)
    RT   Primary education—Curricula, Nonsexist
    NT   Sexism in textbooks (Primary education)
    UF   Primary education—Sexism in curricula

Sexism in curricula (Secondary education)
    RT   Secondary education—Curricula, Nonsexist
    NT   Sexism in textbooks (Secondary education)
    UF   Secondary education—Sexism in curricula

Sexism in educational tests and measurements
    BT   Educational tests and measurements
            Sex discrimination in education

Sexism in employment interviewing
    BT   Women—Employment
    RT   Employment interviewing, Nonsexist
            Job hunting for women
    UF   Employment interviewing, Sexism in

Sexism in gynecology
    BT   Gynecology
            Sexism in medical care
    UF   Gynecology, Sexism in

Sexism in interpersonal relations
    BT   Interpersonal relations
    RT   Interpersonal relations, Nonsexist
    UF   "Double standard"
            Interpersonal relations, Sexism in

Sexism in labor unions
    RT   Labor unionists, Women
            Sex discrimination in labor unions
    UF   Labor unions, Sexism in
            Sexism in trade unions

Sexism in language
    BT   Sociolinguistics

Sexism in language (cont.)
- RT   Androgyny in language
- Men—Language
- Women—Language
- NT   Sexism in language (English)
- UF   Language, Sexism in
- Language and sex role

Sexism in language (English)
- BT   Sexism in language
- NT   Sexism in occupational terminology (English language)
- UF   English language, Sexism in

Sexism in mass media
- BT   Mass media
- Sex role socialization
- RT   Mass media, Nonsexist
- NT   Sexism in advertising
- Sexism in motion pictures
- Sexism in periodicals for women
- Sexism in radio programs
- Sexism in television programs
- UF   Mass media, Sexism in

Sexism in medical care
- BT   Medical care
- RT   Women's health movement
- NT   Rape—Attitudes of medical personnel
- Sexism in gynecology
- UF   Medical care, Sexism in

Sexism in motion pictures
- BT   Motion pictures
- Sexism in mass media
- RT   Motion pictures, Nonsexist
- UF   Motion pictures, Sexism in

Sexism in occupational terminology (English language)
- BT   Occupations—Terminology
- Sexism in language (English)

Sexism in periodicals for women
- BT   Periodicals, Women's
- Sexism in mass media
- UF   Periodicals, Women's (Sexism in)
- Women's periodicals, Sexism in

Sexism in psychoanalysis
- BT   Psychoanalysis
- RT   Feminist psychoanalysis
- Sexism in psychology
- Sexism in psychotherapy
- UF   Psychoanalysis, Sexism in

Sexism in psychology
- BT   Psychology
- RT   Feminist psychology
- Sexism in psychoanalysis
- Sexism in psychotherapy
- Women—Psychology
- UF   Psychology, Sexism in

Sexism in psychotherapy
- BT   Psychotherapy
- RT   Feminist psychotherapy
- Sexism in psychoanalysis
- Sexism in psychology
- UF   Psychotherapy, Sexism in

Sexism in radio programs
- BT   Sexism in mass media
- UF   Programs, Radio (Sexism in)
- Radio programs, Sexism in

Sexism in student life and customs
  BT   Student life and customs
  UF   Student customs, Sexism in
        Student life, Sexism in

Sexism in subject headings
  BT   Subject headings
  RT   Subject headings—Women
  UF   Subject headings, Sexism in

Sexism in television programs
  BT   Sexism in mass media
  UF   Programs, Television (Sexism in)
        Television programs, Sexism in

Sexism in textbooks
  BT   Sex role socialization
        Textbooks
  RT   Teaching materials, Nonsexist
        Textbooks, Nonsexist
  UF   Textbooks, Sexism in

Sexism in textbooks (Higher education)
  BT   Sex role socialization of men
        Sex role socialization of women
        Sexism in curricula (Higher education)

Sexism in textbooks (Primary education)
  BT   Sex role socialization of children
        Sexism in children's literature
        Sexism in curricula (Primary education)

Sexism in textbooks (Secondary education)
  BT   Sex role socialization of children
        Sex role socialization of men
        Sex role socialization of women
        Sexism in children's literature
        Sexism in curricula (Secondary education)

Sexism in the social sciences
  UF   Social sciences, Sexism in

Sexism in trade unions
  USE   Sexism in labor unions

Sexism in vocational guidance
  BT   Sex discrimination in education
        Vocational guidance
  RT   Feminist vocational guidance
        Sex-typing of occupations
        Vocational guidance, Nonsexist
        Vocational guidance for men
        Vocational guidance for women
  UF   Vocational guidance, Sexism in

Sexual adustment surgery
  USE   Transsexual surgery

Sexual behavior (Human)
  USE   Sexuality

Sexual counseling and therapy
  USE   Sex counseling and therapy

Sexual discrimination
  USE   Sex discrimination

Sexual freedom
  BT   Sex customs
  RT   Alternative lifestyles
        Extramarital relations
  NT   Group marriage
        Group sex

Sexual psychology
  USE   Sex (Psychology)

Sexual therapy
  USE   Sex counseling and therapy

Sexuality
  BT   Sex (Psychology)
  NT   Bisexuality
        Extramarital relations
        Heterosexuality
        Homosexuality
        Masturbation
        Orgasm
        Sex counseling and therapy
        Transsexuality
  UF   Human sexuality
        Sexual behavior (Human)

LCSH: Sex *and, under classes of persons, the subdivision* Sexual behavior *(e.g.* Girls—Sexual behavior*). ''Sexuality'' is the term used most often in the literature. Its use as a primary heading, subdivided by classes of persons so that all works on human sexuality are brought together, is recommended. The LCSH subdivision is presently assigned both to works on sexuality and to studies of the sexual behavior of classes of persons under various conditions. The subdivision should be assigned only to such behavioral studies.*

Sexuality—Men
  NT   Homosexuality (Male)
        Masturbation (Male)
        Orgasm (Male)
        SEXUALITY—BOYS; SEXUALITY—MIDDLE AGE MEN and similar
            headings
  UF   Men—Sexuality

Sexuality—Women
  NT   Lesbianism
        Masturbation (Female)
        Orgasm (Female)
        SEXUALITY—GIRLS; SEXUALITY—MIDDLE AGE WOMEN and similar
            headings
  UF   Women—Sexuality

Shelters, Women's
  USE   Women's shelters

Shield (Birth control device)
  USE   Intrauterine contraceptives

Single fathers
  BT   Fathers
        Single men
  RT   Children of single fathers
        Divorced men
        Mother-separated children
        Single-parent adoption
        Single-parent family (Father)
  NT   Teen age single fathers
  UF   Fathers, Single
        Fathers, Unmarried
        Fathers, Unwed
        Unmarried fathers
        Unwed fathers

LCSH: Unmarried fathers

Single fathers, Teen age
  USE   Teen age single fathers

Single men
  BT   Men
        Single people
  NT   Divorced men
        Single fathers
        Widowers
  UF   Bachelors
        Men, Single
        Men, Unmarried
        Unmarried men

LCSH: Bachelors

Single mothers
  BT   Mothers
        Single women
  RT   Children of single parents

LCSH: Unmarried mothers

RT   Divorced women
           Father-separated children
           Single-parent adoption
           Single-parent family (Mother)
NT   Teen age single mothers
UF   Mothers, Single
           Mothers, Unmarried
           Mothers, Unwed
           Unmarried mothers
           Unwed mothers

Single mothers, Teen age
USE   Teen age mothers

Single-parent adoption
BT   Family alternatives
RT   Children adopted by a single parent
           Single fathers
           Single mothers
           Single-parent family
UF   Adoption, One-parent
           Adoption, Single-parent
           One-parent adoption

LC **Single-parent family**
Here are entered works on unmarried parents and on parents who are
single through divorce, desertion, widowhood, single-parent adoption, etc.
BT   Family
           Family alternatives
           Parent and child
RT   Children adopted by a single parent
           Children of divorced parents
           Children of single parents
           Divorced people
           Single-parent adoption
UF   Family, One-parent
           Family, Single-parent
           One-parent family
           Parents without partners

Single-parent family (Father)
BT   Fathers
RT   Divorced men
           Mother-separated children
           Single fathers
           Widowers

Single-parent family (Mother)
BT   Mothers
RT   Divorced women
           Father-separated children
           Single mothers
           Widows

Single parents, Children of
USE   Children of single parents

LC **Single people**
NT   Single men
           Single women
UF   People, Single
           People, Unmarried
           Single persons
           Unmarried people

Single persons
USE   Single people

LC **Single women**
BT   Women
NT   Divorced women

LCSH also makes reference from
Maiden aunts. *Equating unmarried and*
maiden is ridiculous—even when it

Single women (cont.)
  NT   Single mothers
        Widows
  UF   Spinsters
        Unmarried women
        Women, Single
        Women, Unmarried
Single women—Pregnancy
  BT   Pregnancy
Single women—Pregnancy—Psychological aspects
  RT   Pregnancy counseling for single women
Single women, Pregnancy counseling for
  USE   Pregnancy counseling for single women
Sisterhoods
  USE   Monasticism and religious orders for women
Sisters, Catholic
  USE   Nuns, Catholic
Sisters, Christian
  USE   Nuns, Christian
LC **Slavery in the United States**
  NT   Abolitionists
LC **Slavery in the United States—Anti-slavery movements**
  UF   Anti-slavery movements (United States)
Slavery in the United States—Anti-slavery movements—Women's activities
  NT   Abolitionists, Women
  UF   Women in the anti-slavery movement (United States)
Slavery in the United States—Condition of slaves
  USE   Slavery in the United States—Treatment of slaves
LC **Slavery in the United States—Fugitive slaves**
  NT   Slavery in the United States—Fugitive women slaves
  UF   Fugitive slaves in the United States
Slavery in the United States—Fugitive women slaves
  BT   Slavery in the United States—Fugitive slaves
        Slavery in the United States—Women slaves
  UF   Slavery in the United States—Women slaves, Fugitive
Slavery in the United States—Treatment of slaves
  NT   Slavery in the United States—Treatment of women slaves
  UF   Slavery in the United States—Condition of slaves
Slavery in the United States—Treatment of women household slaves
  BT   Slavery in the United States—Treatment of women slaves
  UF   "Mammies" (Slavery in the United States)
Slavery in the United States—Treatment of women slaves
  BT   Slavery in the United States—Treatment of slaves
        Slavery in the United States—Women slaves
  NT   Slavery in the United States—Treatment of women household
          slaves
  UF   Slavery in the United States—Women slaves—Treatment
Slavery in the United States—Women slaves
  NT   Slavery in the United States—Fugitive women slaves
        Slavery in the United States—Treatment of women slaves
  UF   Slaves, Women (United States)
        Women slaves (United States)
Slavery in the United States—Women slaves—Personal narratives
Slavery in the United States—Women slaves—Treatment
  USE   Slavery in the United States—Treatment of women slaves
Slavery in the United States—Women slaves, Fugitive
  USE   Slavery in the United States—Fugitive women slaves
Slaves, Women (United States)
  USE   Slavery in the United States—Women slaves

comes to aunts. *Recommend deleting* LCSH Aunts *and* Maiden aunts *and substituting* Aunts and Uncles. *The present headings, and the one proposed, are assigned primarily to juvenile works, often with the subdivision* Fiction. *(LCSH does not have a heading for uncles despite justification for such a heading in the literature.)*

LCSH uses subdivision Condition of slaves.

LCSH: Mammies

Small presses
- BT   Publishers and publishing
- RT   Women's presses
- UF   Little presses
  Publishers and publishing, Small press

Social alienation
- USE   Alienation (Social psychology)

Social insurance
- USE   Social security

Social movements
- NT   Gay liberation movement
  Men's liberation
  Women's movement (1960–   )

Social planning
- USE   Social policy

LC **Social policy**
- NT   Women's movement (1960–   ) and social policy
- UF   National planning
  Planning, National
  Planning, State
  Public policy
  Social planning
  State planning

LC **Social role**
- RT   Sex role
- NT   Role models
  Role reversal

Social sciences, Sexism in
- USE   Sexism in the social sciences

LC **Social security**
- NT   Medicare
  Sex discrimination in pension and social security benefits
- UF   Insurance, Social
  Insurance, State and compulsory
  Old age, survivors, and disability insurance
  Social insurance
  State and insurance

Social workers (Volunteer)
- BT   Volunteer work and workers
- NT   Social workers (Volunteer), Women
- UF   Volunteer social workers

Social workers (Volunteer), Women   *LCSH:* Women volunteers in social
- BT   Social workers (Volunteer)   service
- UF   Women in social work (Volunteer)
  Women social workers (Volunteer)

Socialism and Feminism
- USE   Feminism and socialism

Socialism and women   *LCSH:* Women and socialism
Here are entered general works on women's roles and life in socialist
societies. Works on women socialists are entered under SOCIALISTS, WOMEN;
works on the socialist interpretation of women's oppression are entered
under FEMINISM, SOCIALIST.
- RT   Feminism, Socialist
  Socialists, Women
- UF   Marxism and women
  Women and Marxism
  Women and Socialism

Socialist feminism
- UF   Feminism, Socialist

Socialists, Women
- cf.   note under SOCIALISM AND WOMEN

Socialists, Women (cont.)
    RT   Feminism, Socialist
             Socialism and women
    UF   Marxist women
             Women Marxists
             Women Socialists

LC **Socialization**
    NT   Sex role socialization
    UF   Enculturation

Sociolinguistics
    NT   Androgyny in language
             Sexism in language

Soldiers, Women   *LCSH:* Women soldiers
    NT   UNITED STATES—ARMED FORCES—WOMEN; UNITED STATES. MARINE CORPS—WOMEN MARINES and similar headings under names of countries
    UF   Women soldiers

Sons and fathers
    USE   Fathers and sons

Sons and mothers
    USE   Mothers and sons

Sorcery
    USE   Witchcraft

Spanish-American women—United States
    USE   Latino women—United States

Sperm banks
    RT   Artificial insemination, Human
    UF   Banks, Sperm
             Semen banks

Spinsters
    USE   Single women

Spirituality, Feminist
    USE   Feminist spirituality

Spontaneous abortion
    USE   Miscarriage

LC **Sports**
    NT   SPORTS FOR CHILDREN; SPORTS FOR MEN; SPORTS FOR WOMEN; etc.
    UF   Field sports

LC **Sports for children**
    BT   Sports
    UF   Children—Sports

Sports for men   *LCSH:* Sports
    BT   Sports
    UF   Men—Sports

LC **Sports for women**
    BT   Sports
             Women—Health
    UF   Women—Sports

State and insurance
    USE   Social security

LC **State governments—Officials and employees**
    BT   Public officials
    RT   Local officials and employees
    UF   State officials and employees

State governments—Officials and employees, Women
    BT   Women—Employment

State legislation and the Equal Rights Amendment (Proposed)
    USE   Equal Rights Amendment (Proposed) and State legislation

State officials and employees
    USE   State governments—Officials and employees

State planning
    USE   Economic policy
             Social policy

Status of athletics coaches (Women)
    USE   Athletics coaches, Women—Status

Status of businesswomen
    USE   Businesswomen—Status

Status of counselors (Women)
    USE   Counselors, Women—Status

Status of office workers (Women)
    USE   Office workers, Women—Status

Status of women athletics coaches
    USE   Athletics coaches, Women—Status

Status of women counselors
    USE   Counselors, Women—Status

Status of women in business
    USE   Businesswomen—Status

Status of women in the professions
    USE   Professional women—Status

Status of women office workers
    USE   Office workers, Women—Status

Stenographers
    BT   Office workers
    NT   Stenographers, Women

Stenographers, Women
    BT   Stenographers
    UF   Women stenographers

Stereotyping of occupations
    USE   Sex-typing of occupations

LC **Sterilization (Birth control)**
    BT   Birth control
    NT   Sterilization of men (Birth control)
            Sterilization of women (Birth control)

Sterilization of men (Birth control)
    BT   Sterilization (Birth control)
    RT   Artificial insemination, Human
    NT   Vasectomy
    UF   Male sterilization (Human)
            Men—Sterilization

Sterilization of women (Birth control)
    BT   Sterilization (Birth control)
    RT   Sterilization of women (Involuntary)
    NT   Hysterectomy
            Laparoscopy
            Tubal ligation (Birth control)
    UF   Female sterilization (Human)
            Women—Sterilization

LCSH: Sterilization of women

Sterilization of women (Involuntary)
    BT   Violence against women
            Women—Civil rights
    RT   Sterilization of women (Birth control)
    UF   Female sterilization (Human)
            Women—Sterilization

LCSH: Sterilization of women. *"Notably in ghetto areas [hospitals] tend to do many, and not entirely voluntary, sterilizations. Black women in the South are all too familiar with the 'Mississippi Appendectomy' in which their fallopian tubes are tied or their uterus is removed without their knowing it."* Our bodies, ourselves (1973)

Stores, Retail—Employees
    USE   Clerks (Retail trade)

Streetwalkers
    USE   Prostitutes

LC **Student aspirations (Indirect)**
    UF   Aspirations, Student
            Educational aspirations
            Student plans

Student aspirations—African-American women
    BT   Student aspirations—Women students—United States
    UF   African-American women students—Aspirations

Student aspirations—Women students (Indirect)
    RT   Women—Education—Role conflict and the subdivision ROLE
            CONFLICT under similar headings.

Student aspirations—Women students—United States
    NT   Student aspirations—African-American [JEWISH-AMERICAN, ETC.]
            women

Student customs, Sexism in
  USE   Sexism in student life and customs

Student life, Sexism in
  USE   Sexism in student life and customs

Student life and customs   *LCSH:* Students
    BT   Students
    NT   Sexism in student life and customs
    UF   School life

Student guidance
  USE   Vocational guidance

Student plans
  USE   Student aspirations

LC **Students**
    NT   Student life and customs

Studies of women
  USE   Women's studies

Study, Courses of
  USE   Education—Curricula

LC **Subject headings**
Here are entered general works on subject headings and lists of subject
headings in the English language.
    NT   Homophobia in subject headings
            Sexism in subject headings
    UF   Headings, Subject
            Indexing vocabularies
            Subject headings, English
            Thesauri, Subject

LC **Subject headings—Homosexuals and homosexuality**
    RT   Homophobia in subject headings
    UF   Homosexuality—Subject headings
            Homosexuals—Subject headings

LC **Subject headings—Women**
    RT   Sexism in subject headings
    UF   Women—Subject headings

Subject headings, English
  USE   Subject headings

Subject headings, Homophobia in
  USE   Homophobia in subject headings

Subject headings, Sexism in
  USE   Sexism in subject headings

Suckling (Infant feeding)
  USE   Breast feeding

LC **Suffrage**
    NT   Women—Suffrage

Suffrage—Women
  USE   Women—Suffrage

Suffragists
    BT   Feminists
    RT   Women—Suffrage
    UF   Women—Suffrage—Biography

LC **Support (Domestic relations)**
    RT   Desertion and nonsupport
            Married men—Legal status, laws, etc.
            Runaway wives, husbands, etc.
    NT   Alimony
            Child support (Law)

Surnames
    USE   Names, Personal

Swingers and swinging (Sex customs)
    USE   Swinging and swingers (Sex customs)

Swinging and swingers (Sex customs)
    BT   Group sex
            Marriage alternatives
    UF   Swingers and swinging (Sex customs)

Switching roles
    USE   Role reversal

LC **Teachers**
    NT   Nuns—Employment in public schools

LC **Teachers—Attitudes**
    NT   Women—Education—Attitudes of teachers

Teaching—Aids and devices
    USE   Teaching materials

Teaching materials
    NT   Textbooks
    UF   Educational media
            Instructional materials
            Teaching—Aids and devices

LCSH: Teaching—Aids and devices

Teaching materials, Nonsexist
    BT   Education—Curricula, Nonsexist
    RT   Sexism in textbooks
    NT   Children's films, Nonsexist
            Children's literature, Nonsexist
            Textbooks, Nonsexist
    UF   Nonsexist teaching materials

LC **Technology—Social aspects**
    NT   Automation—Social aspects
            Technology and women's employment

Technology and women's employment
Here are entered works on the effect of technology on routine work tasks
traditionally performed by women.
    BT   Technology—Social aspects
            Women—Employment
    NT   Automation and women's employment

Teen age
    NT   Teen age men
            Teen age women
    UF   Adolescence
            Youth

Teen age and employment
Here are entered works on teen age as a factor in finding and keeping
suitable employment.
    BT   Age and employment
    RT   Labor supply (Teen age)
            Teen agers—Employment
    UF   Employment and youth
            Employment and teen age

LCSH: Youth, Young men, Young
women. *Recommend* Teen age, Teen
age men, Teen age women. *The LCSH
cross reference clearly reveals that
LC's intention was to substitute youth
for teen age. However, since "youth"
and "young" are not specific, the
headings were often misapplied. For
example, Susan Stern's* With the
Weathermen *(1975) was assigned the
heading* Youth—United States—
Political activity; *Stern was 24 years
old when she joined SDS in 1967; her
associates were of comparable age.*

Teen age and employment—Women
    BT   Teen age women—Employment
    RT   Sex discrimination in employment—Teen age women

Teen age and unemployment
    USE   Labor supply (Teen age)

Teen age fathers
    BT   Fathers
    RT   Teen age marriage
    NT   Teen age single fathers
    UF   Fathers, Teen age

LC **Teen age marriage**
    BT   Marriage
    RT   Teen age fathers
             Teen age mothers
    UF   Early marriage
             Marriage, Teen age

Teen age men   *LCSH:* Young men
    BT   Men
             Teen age
    NT   Juvenile delinquents (Male)
    UF   Men, Teen age

Teen age men—Crime
    USE   Juvenile delinquents (Male)

Teen age men—Sex role socialization
    USE   Sex role socialization of men

Teen age men, Delinquent
    USE   Juvenile delinquents (Male)

Teen age men authors
    USE   Authors, Teen age men

Teen age mothers
    BT   Mothers
    RT   Teen age marriage
    NT   Teen age single mothers
    UF   Mothers, Teen age

Teen age single fathers
    BT   Single fathers
             Teen age fathers
    UF   Single fathers, Teen age

Teen age single mothers
    BT   Single mothers
             Teen age mothers
    UF   Single mothers, Teen age

Teen age women   *LCSH:* Young women
    BT   Teen age
             Women
    NT   Juvenile delinquents (Female)
             Jewish teen age women
    UF   Women, Teen age

Teen age women—Counseling
    USE   Counseling for teen age women

Teen age women—Crime
    USE   Juvenile delinquents (Female)

Teen age women—Education   *LCSH:* Education of women
    BT   Women—Education
    RT   Education, Secondary—Curricula, Nonsexist
    UF   Education—Teen age women

Teen age women—Employment
    BT   Teen agers-Employment
    NT   Sex discrimination in employment—Teen age women
             Teen age and employment—Women

Teen age women—Employment, Sex discrimination in
  USE   Sex discrimination in employment—Teen age women

Teen age women—Occupation, Choice of
  USE   Vocational guidance for teen age women

Teen age women—Pregnancy
  BT   Pregnancy
  UF   Pregnancy and teen age
        Pregnant teen agers

          LCSH: Pregnant schoolgirls

Teen age women—Pregnancy—Psychological aspects
  RT   Pregnancy counseling for teen age women

Teen age women—Sex discrimination in employment
  USE   Sex discrimination in employment—Teen age women

Teen age women—Sex role socialization
  USE   Sex role socialization of women

Teen age women—Sexuality
  USE   Sexuality—Teen age women

Teen age women—Vocational guidance
  USE   Vocational guidance for teen age women

Teen age women, Counseling for
  USE   Counseling for teen age women

Teen age women, Delinquent
  USE   Juvenile delinquents (Female)

Teen age women, Pregnancy counseling for
  USE   Pregnancy counseling for teen age women

Teen age women authors
  USE   Authors, Teen age women

Teen age women's projects and services
  BT   Women's projects and services
  RT   Counseling for teen age women
  UF   Teen age women's services

Teen age women's services
  USE   Teen age women's projects and services

Teen agers—Employment
  RT   Labor supply (Teen age)
        Teen age and employment
  NT   Teen age women—Employment

Teen agers in the labor force
  USE   Labor supply (Teen age)

Teen agers in the labor market
  USE   Labor supply (Teen age)

Television programs, Sexism in
  USE   Sexism in television programs

Tension, Premenstrual
  USE   Premenstrual tension

Tests and measurements in education
  USE   Educational tests and measurements

Textbooks
  BT   Teaching materials
  NT   Textbooks, Nonsexist
        Sexism in textbooks
  UF   School books

Textbooks, Nonsexist
  BT   Teaching materials, Nonsexist
        Textbooks
  RT   Sexism in textbooks
  UF   Nonsexist textbooks

Textbooks, Sexism in
  USE   Sexism in textbooks

Theological anthropology
  USE   Man and woman (Theology)

Theological anthropology (Biblical)
  USE   Man and woman (Christian theology)
         Man and woman (Jewish theology)

Therapy and counseling, Feminist
  USE   Feminist counseling and therapy

Thesauri, Subject
  USE   Subject headings

Trade
  USE   Business

LC **Trade and professional associations**
      RT   Professional unions
      UF   Professional associations

Trade and professional associations—Women's caucuses
      UF   Women's caucuses—Trade and professional associations

Trade unions
  USE   Labor unions

Trades
  USE   Occupations

Training, Occupational
  USE   Occupational training

Training, Vocational
  USE   Occupational training

Training of children
  USE   Children—Development and guidance

Training of employees
  USE   Employees, Training of

Training within industry
  USE   Employees, Training of

Transethnic adoption
  USE   Interethnic adoption

Transethnic family
  USE   Interethnic family

Transethnic marriage
  USE   Interethnic marriage

Transexuality
  USE   Transsexuality

Transnational adoption
  USE   International adoption

Transracial adoption
  USE   Interracial adoption

Transracial family
  USE   Interracial family

Transracial marriage
  USE   Interracial marriage

Transsexual surgery
      RT   Transsexuality
      UF   Change of sex   *LCSH:* Change of sex
            Sex change
            Sexual adjustment surgery

Transsexuality
      BT   Sex role
            Sexuality
      RT   Transsexual surgery
      UF   Sex role inversion
            Transexuality

Transvestism
- BT   Sex role
- RT   Manhood (Psychology)
        Transvestites
        Womanhood (Psychology)
- UF   Cross-dressing

Transvestites
- RT   Transvestism

Trial marriage
- USE   Unmarried couples

Tubal ligation (Birth control)
- BT   Sterilization of women (Birth control)
- RT   Laparoscopy
- UF   Tube-tying (Birth control)

Tube-tying (Birth control)
- USE   Tubal ligation (Birth control)

Two-step marriage
- USE   Unmarried couples

Typists
- BT   Office workers

Typists, Women
- UF   Women typists

Uncles
- USE   Aunts and uncles

Unemployment
- USE   Labor supply

Unemployment and teen age
- USE   Labor supply (Teen age)

Unemployment and women
- USE   Labor supply (Women)

Unions, Labor
- USE   Labor unions

Unions, Professional
- USE   Professional unions

Unions, White collar
- USE   Labor unions

Unisexuality
- USE   Androgyny

LC **United States—Armed forces—Women**
- BT   Soldiers, Women

United States. Constitution. Equal rights amendment (Proposed)
- USE   Equal rights amendment (Proposed)

LC **United States. Marine Corps—Women marines**
- BT   Soldiers, Women

LC **Universities and colleges**
- RT   Higher education; cf. note under HIGHER EDUCATION
- UF   Colleges

Universities and colleges—Curricula
- USE   Higher education—Curricula

LC **Universities and colleges—Health services**

Universities and colleges—Health services for women
- BT   Women's health centers and clinics
- RT   Universities and colleges—Women's centers

Universities and colleges—Nonsexist curricula
- USE   Higher education—Curricula, Nonsexist

Universities and colleges—Sexism in curricula
- USE   Sexism in curricula (Higher education)

Universities and colleges—Women's centers
- BT   Women's centers and networks
- RT   Universities and colleges—Health services for women
- UF   Universities and colleges—Women's networks

Universities and colleges—Women's networks
- USE   Universities and colleges—Women's centers

University graduates
- USE   College graduates

Unmarried couples
- BT   Extramarital relations
         Marriage alternatives
- RT   Children of unmarried couples
- NT   Common law marriage
         Contractual marriage
- UF   Cohabitation
         Couples, Unmarried
         Marriage, Trial
         Marriage, Two-step
         Trial marriage
         Two-step marriage

Unmarried couples, Children of
- USE   Children of unmarried couples

Unmarried fathers
- USE   Single fathers

Unmarried men
- USE   Single men

Unmarried mothers
- USE   Single mothers

Unmarried parents
- USE   Single parents

Unmarried parents, Children of
- USE   Children of single parents
         Children of unmarried couples

Unmarried people
- USE   Single people

Unmarried women
- USE   Single women

Unwed fathers
- USE   Single fathers

Unwed mothers
- USE   Single mothers

Vaginal diaphragms
- USE   Diaphragm (Birth control device)

LC **Vasectomy**
- BT   Sterilization of men (Birth control)

Vasectomy—Psychological aspects
- RT   Vasectomy counseling

Vasectomy clinics and referral services
- BT   Birth control clinics
- RT   Vasectomy counseling

Vasectomy counseling
- BT   Counseling for men
- RT   Vasectomy—Psychological aspects
         Vasectomy clinics and referral services

Vatican Council, 2d, 1962–1965 and women
- BT   Catholic Church and women
- UF   Women and the Vatican Council, 2d, 1962–1965

LC **Vietnamese conflict, 1961–1975—Protest movements**
- UF   Anti-war protest movements (1961–1975)

UF   Peace Movement (1961–1975)
       Protest Movements, Anti-war (1961–1975)

Vietnamese conflict, 1961–1975—Protest movements, Women's
  RT   Feminism and pacifism
  NT   Names of specific organizations; e.g. WOMEN STRIKE FOR PEACE,
        ANOTHER MOTHER FOR PEACE, etc.
  UF   Vietnamese conflict, 1961–1975—Women's anti-war protest
        movements (1961–1975)
       Women's peace movements (1961–1975)
       Women's protest movements (Anti-war) (1961–1975)

Vietnamese conflict, 1961–1975—Women's protest movements
  USE Vietnamese conflict, 1961–1975—Protest movements, Women's

LC **Violence**
  RT   Aggressiveness (Psychology)
  NT   Household violence
       Violence against women

Violence, Household
  USE Household violence

Violence against women
  BT   Offenses against the person
       Violence
  NT   Rape
       Sterilization of women (Involuntary)
       Woman battering
  UF   Women, Violence against

Violence in the home
  USE Household violence

Vocation, Choice of
  USE Vocational guidance

LC **Vocational education**
  cf.   note under EMPLOYEES, TRAINING OF
  BT   Education
       Human resources policy
  RT   Occupational retraining
       Occupational training
  NT   Vocational guidance
  UF   Career education
       Education, Vocational

LC **Vocational guidance**
  BT   Counseling
       Vocational education
  RT   Occupational retraining
       Occupational training
  NT   Feminist vocational guidance
       Sexism in vocational guidance
       Vocational guidance, Nonsexist
       Vocational guidance for men
       Vocational guidance for women
       BUSINESS—VOCATIONAL GUIDANCE; COUNSELING—VOCATIONAL
         GUIDANCE and the subdivision VOCATIONAL GUIDANCE under the
         names of other occupations and professions.
  UF   Business, Choice of
       Careers
       Guidance, Student
       Guidance, Vocational
       Jobs
       Occupations, Choice of
       Professions, Choice of
       Student guidance
       Vocation, Choice of
       Vocational opportunities

Vocational guidance, Feminist
  USE   Feminist vocational guidance

Vocational guidance, Nonsexist
  BT   Vocational guidance
  RT   Feminist vocational guidance
         Sex-typing of occupations
         Sexism in vocational guidance
         Vocational guidance for men
         Vocational guidance for women
  UF   Nonsexist vocational guidance

Vocational guidance, Sexism in
  USE   Sexism in vocational guidance

Vocational guidance for girls
  BT   Counseling for girls
         Vocational guidance for women
  UF   Girls—Occupation, Choice of
         Girls—Vocational guidance

Vocational guidance for men
  BT   Vocational guidance
  RT   Sex-typing of occupations
         Sexism in vocational guidance
         Vocational guidance, Nonsexist
  UF   Men—Occupation, Choice of
         Men—Vocational guidance

Vocational guidance for teen age women
  BT   Counseling for teen age women
         Vocational guidance for women
  UF   Teen age women—Occupation, Choice of
         Teen age women—Vocational guidance

Vocational guidance for women
  BT   Counseling for women
         Vocational guidance
         Women—Employment
  RT   Feminist vocational guidance
         Occupational training for women
         Sex-typing of occupations
         Sexism in vocational guidance
         Vocational guidance, Nonsexist
  NT   Vocational guidance for girls
         Vocational guidance for teen age women
         Vocational guidance for women reentering employment
  UF   Women—Occupation, Choice of
         Women—Vocational guidance

Vocational guidance for women reentering employment
  BT   Counseling for middle age women
         Counseling for senior women
         Vocational guidance for women
  RT   College graduate women—Employment reentry
         Occupational retraining for women
         Women—Employment reentry
  UF   Middle age women—Vocational guidance
         Senior women—Vocational guidance
         Women—Occupation, Choice of
         Women—Vocational guidance

Vocational opportunities
  USE   Vocational guidance

Vocational retraining
  USE   Occupational retraining

Vocational training
  USE   Occupational training

Volunteer church workers
 USE Church workers (Volunteer)

Volunteer social workers
 USE Social workers (Volunteer)

Volunteer work and feminism
 USE Feminism and volunteerism

Volunteer work and workers
 NT Church workers (Volunteer)
   Social workers (Volunteer)
   Volunteer workers, Women

Volunteer workers, Women
 BT Volunteer work and workers
 RT Feminism and volunteerism
 NT Church workers (Volunteer), Women
   Social workers (Volunteer), Women
 UF Women volunteer workers
   Women workers, Volunteer

Volunteerism and feminism
 USE Feminism and volunteerism

LC **Wages**
 NT Equal pay for equal work
 UF Compensation
   Workers—Wages

Wages—Household workers
 RT Household workers

Wages—Women
 RT Women—Employment
 NT Sex discrimination in wages
   Wages for housework movement
 UF Women—Wages

Wages, Sex discrimination in
 USE Sex discrimination in wages

Wages for housework movement
 BT Wages—Women
 RT Housewives
 UF Housework movement, Wages for
   Paid housework movement
   Pay for housework movement

War—Civilians' work
 BT War—Human resources
 NT WORLD WAR, 1939–1945—CIVILIANS' WORK and similar headings
    under names of wars
 UF Civilians' work in war-time
   Defense work in war-time, Civilian
   War work

War—Civilians' work—Women
 BT Women—Employment
 RT War and women
 UF War—Women's work
   Women—Civilian work in war-time
   Women—Employment in war-time
   Women in war-time
   Women's work in war-time

War—Human resources   *LCSH:* War—Manpower
 NT War—Civilians' work

War—Women's work
 USE War—Civilians' work—Women

War and women
Here are entered works on women's psychological reaction to war and on

War and women (cont.)
women as victims of war. For works on women's work during war-time
see WAR—CIVILIANS' WORK—WOMEN; WORLD WAR, 1939–1945—CIVILIANS'
WORK—WOMEN and similar headings under names of wars.
    RT   War—Civilians' work—Women
          World War, 1939–1945—Civilians' work—Women
    UF   Women and war
          Women in war-time

War work
    USE   War—Civilians' work

Way of life, Jewish
    USE   Jews—Social life and customs

White collar unions
    USE   Labor unions

White collar workers
    BT   Working classes—Employment
    NT   Clerks (Retail trade)
          Office workers
          Sales personnel

LC **Widowers**
    BT   Single men
    RT   Single-parent family (Father)
    NT   Remarriage

LC **Widows**
    BT   Single women
    RT   Single-parent family (Mother)
    NT   Remarriage

Widows—Legal status, laws, etc.
    RT   Married women—Legal status, laws, etc.

Wife and husband
    USE   Husband and wife

LC **Wife battering**
    BT   Woman battering
          Interpersonal relations in marriage
    UF   Battered wives
          Wife beating

Wife beating
    USE   Wife battering

LC **Witchcraft**
    RT   Feminist wicce and wicceans
          Witches
    UF   Sorcery

Witches
    BT   Women in folklore and mythology
    RT   Feminist wicce and wicceans
          Witchcraft

Witches, Feminist
    USE   Feminist wicce and wicceans

Wives
    USE   Married women
          ARMY WIVES; CLERGYMEN'S WIVES; PRESIDENTS—U.S.—WIVES;
              RUNAWAY WIVES, HUSBANDS, ETC. and similar headings.

Wives, Runaway
    USE   Runaway wives, husbands, etc.

Woman
    USE   Women

Woman (Christian theology)
    BT   Man and woman (Christian theology)
          Woman (Theology)
    RT   Christianity and women
          Religious life (Christianity)—Women

Woman (Jewish theology)
- BT   Man and woman (Jewish theology)
       Woman (Theology)
- RT   Judaism and women
       Religious life (Judaism)—Women

Woman (Theology)
- BT   Man and woman (Theology)
- RT   Religion and women
       Religious life—Women
- NT   Woman (Christian theology)
       Woman (Jewish theology)

Woman battering
- BT   Household violence
       Violence against women
- RT   Child battering
- NT   Wife battering
- UF   Assault, Criminal (Against women)
       Battered women
       Criminal assault against women
       Women battering

LCSH: Wife beating. *Not all of the battered women are married to the men doing the battering. Both headings are needed since the options open to married and single women, and to women related in nonconjugal ways to the batterer, are different.*

Woman battering—Law and legislation
- RT   Anti-woman-battering movement

Woman battering—Law reform movement
- USE Anti-woman-battering movement

Woman battering—Psychological aspects
- BT   Men—Psychology
       Women—Psychology

Woman battering—Self help and law reform movement
- USE Anti-woman-battering movement

Womanhood (Psychology)
- BT   Sex (Psychology)
       Women—Psychology
- RT   Androgyny
       Transvestism
- UF   Feminine mystique
       Femininity (Psychology)

LCSH: Femininity (Psychology). *Femininity—even with the (Psychology) gloss—conjures up the "white-glove syndrome." Masculinity (Psychology) conjures up an equally false image.* Manhood (Psychology) *and* Womanhood *(Psychology) are neutral and recommended.*

Womanpower
- USE Human resources

Womanspirit
- USE Feminist spirituality

LC **Women (Indirect)**
Here are entered general works on women. Works on women in specific age groups are entered under GIRLS, TEEN AGE WOMEN, MIDDLE AGE WOMEN, SENIOR WOMEN as appropriate.
- NT   Criminals, Women
       Feminism
       Girls
       Lesbians
       Married women
       Middle age women
       Mothers
       Prostitutes (Female)
       Senior women
       Single women
       Senior women
       Teen age women
       Working class women
       CHRISTIAN WOMEN; JEWISH WOMEN and similar headings
- UF   Female
       Woman

Women—Academic counseling
  USE   Academic counseling for women

Women—Achievement motivation and sex role
  USE   Achievement motivation and sex role of women

Women—Adult education
  BT   Adult education
  UF   Adult education—Women
       Middle age women—Education
       Senior women—Education
       Women—Education, Adult

Women—Affirmative action
  USE   Affirmative action for women

Women—Anatomy
  USE   Human anatomy (Female)

Women—Biography
  NT   Subdivision BIOGRAPHY under names of occupations, areas of
       activity, and classes of women; e.g. SOLDIERS, WOMEN; LABOR
       UNIONISTS, WOMEN; JEWISH WOMEN

Women—Career-family conflict
  USE   Women—Education—Role conflict
        Women—Employment—Role conflict

Women—Civil rights (Indirect)   *LCSH:* Women's rights
  BT   Civil rights
  RT   Feminism
       Women—Legal status, laws, etc.
       Women's movement (1960–   )
  NT   Affirmative action for women
       Child care
       Girls—Rights
       Sex discrimination
       Sterilization of women (Involuntary)
       Women—Suffrage
  UF   Civil rights—Women
       Emancipation of women
       Rights of women
       Women—Emancipation
       Women's rights

Women—Civil rights—United States
  RT   Women—Legal status, laws, etc.—United States
  NT   Equal rights amendment (Proposed)

Women—Civilian work in war-time
  USE   War—Civilians' work—Women

Women—Clubs
  USE   Women's organizations

Women—Counseling
  USE   Counseling for women

Women—Crime
  USE   Criminals, Women

Women—Diseases
  BT   Women—Health
  RT   Gynecology
  NT   Breast cancer

LC **Women—Economic conditions**
  NT   Poor women

Women—Education (Indirect)   *LCSH:* Education of women
  BT   Education
  RT   Education—Curricula, Nonsexist
  NT   Coeducation
       Education and income—Women
       Educational opportunity and women's status

　　NT　Girls—Education
　　　　Minority women—Education
　　　　Teen age women—Education
　　　　WOMEN—ADULT EDUCATION; WOMEN—HIGHER EDUCATION and similar
　　　　　　headings for specific types of education
　　UF　Education—Women
Women—Education—Attitudes of teachers
　　BT　Teachers—Attitudes
　　RT　Women—Education—Role conflict
Women—Education—Counseling
　　USE　Academic counseling for women
Women—Education—Nonsexist counseling
　　USE　Academic counseling, Nonsexist
Women—Education—Role conflict
　　BT　Sex role conflict
　　RT　Academic counseling, Nonsexist
　　　　Student aspirations—Women students
　　　　Sexism in academic counseling
　　　　Women—Education—Attitudes of teachers
　　UF　Career-family conflict, Women's
　　　　Family-career conflict, Women's
　　　　Marriage-career conflict, Women's
　　　　Women—Career-family conflict
　　　　Women—Education—Sex role conflict
　　　　Women—Family-career conflict
　　　　Women—Marriage-career conflict
Women—Education—Sex role conflict
　　USE　Women—Education—Role conflict
Women—Education—Sexism in counseling
　　USE　Sexism in academic counseling
Women—Education—United States
　　NT　Minority women—Education—United States
Women—Education, Adult
　　USE　Women—Adult education
Women—Education, Higher
　　USE　Women—Higher education
Women—Emancipation
　　USE　Women—Civil rights
LC **Women—Employment (Indirect)**
　　RT　Labor supply (Women)
　　　　Wages—Women
　　NT　Age and employment—Women
　　　　Age discrimination in employment—Women
　　　　Child care leave (Mother)
　　　　College graduate women—Employment
　　　　Employees (Women), Training of
　　　　Employment interviewing, Nonsexist
　　　　Married women—Employment
　　　　Minority women—Employment
　　　　Mothers—Employment
　　　　Nuns—Employment
　　　　Occupations, Women's
　　　　Sex discrimination in employment
　　　　Sexism in employment interviewing
　　　　Technology and women's employment
　　　　Vocational guidance for women
　　　　War—Civilians' work—Women
　　　　Workers, Women
　　　　AGRICULTURISTS, WOMEN; HOUSEHOLD WORKERS, WOMEN; LOCAL
　　　　　　OFFICIALS AND EMPLOYEES, WOMEN; OFFICE WORKERS, WOMEN and
　　　　　　similar headings under names of specific types of employment

Women—Employment (Indirect) (cont.)
  UF   Employment—Women
        Women—Occupations
        Women workers

Women—Employment—Absenteeism
  USE Absenteeism (Labor)—Women

Women—Employment—Attitudes of employers
  BT   Attitudes (Psychology)
  RT   Sexism in employment
  UF   Employers' attitudes towards women workers

Women—Employment—Attitudes of men
  BT   Attitudes (Psychology)
  RT   Sexism in employment
  UF   Men's attitudes toward women coworkers
        Workers' attitudes toward women coworkers

Women—Employment—Job satisfaction
  BT   Job satisfaction
  RT   Absenteeism (Labor)—Women

Women—Employment—Law and legislation
  USE Labor laws and legislation—Women

Women—Employment—Legal aspects
  RT   Labor laws and legislation—Women
  NT   Affirmative action for women; cf. note under AFFIRMATIVE ACTION
        FOR WOMEN

Women—Employment—Role conflict
  BT   Sex role conflict
  RT   Women—Employment—Self-attitude
  UF   Career-family conflict, Women's
        Family-career conflict, Women's
        Marriage-career conflict, Women's
        Women—Career-family conflict
        Women—Employment—Sex role conflict
        Women—Family-career conflict
        Women—Marriage-career conflict

Women—Employment—Self attitude
  BT   Attitudes (Psychology)
  RT   Women—Employment—Role conflict
        Sexism in employment
  UF   Women workers' attitudes towards work
        Women's attitudes towards work

Women—Employment—Sex role conflict
  USE Women—Employment—Role conflict

Women—Employment—United States
  NT   Minority women—Employment—United States

Women—Employment, Part-time
  USE Women—part-time employment

Women—Employment in war-time
  USE War—Civilians' work—Women

Women—Employment reentry
  RT   Middle age and employment—Women
        Occupational retraining for women
        Seniors and employment—Women
        Vocational guidance for women reentering employment
  UF   Displaced housewives
        Reentry into employment, Women's
        Women—Reentry into employment

Women—Enfranchisement
  USE Suffrage—Women

Women—Family-career conflict
  USE Women—Education—Role conflict
        Women—Employment—Role conflict

Women—Frontier and pioneer life
  USE   Frontier and pioneer life of women

Women—Grooming
  USE   Grooming for women

Women—Health
  BT   Health
  RT   Women's health movement
  NT   Body awareness training for women
       Sports for women
       Women—Diseases
       MIDDLE AGE WOMEN—HEALTH, TEEN AGE WOMEN—HEALTH and
         similar headings

Women—Higher education
  BT   Higher education
  RT   Higher education—Curricula, Nonsexist
       Women's studies
  UF   Higher education—Women
       Women—Education, Higher

LCSH: Higher education of women

Women—Higher education—Graduate work
  BT   Higher education—Graduate work

Women—Higher education—Honors courses
  BT   Education, Higher—Honors courses

LC **Women—History**
      To 500
      Middle ages, 500–1500
      Renaissance, 1450–1600
      Modern period, 1600–1900
      Twentieth century, 1900–
  NT   Feminism—History
       Women's resistance and revolts
  UF   Herstory

The date subdivisions suggested apply only to Western culture.

Women—Homosexuality
  USE   Lesbianism

Women—In-service training
  USE   Employees (Women), Training of

Women—Language
  RT   Sexism and language

LC **Women—Legal status, laws, etc. (Indirect)**
  RT   Women—Civil rights
  NT   Labor laws and legislation—Women
       Lesbians—Legal status, laws, etc.
       Married women—Legal status, laws, etc.
       Prostitutes (Female)—Legal status, laws, etc.
       Sex discrimination—Law and legislation
  UF   Legal status of women

Women—Legal status, laws, etc.—Discriminatory legislation
  NT   Labor laws and legislation, Discriminatory—Women
       Prostitution—Law and legislation, Discriminatory
       Rape—Law and legislation, Discriminatory
  UF   Discrimination in law and legislation, Sex
       Law, Sex discrimination in
       Protective law and legislation (Women)
       Sex discrimination in law and legislation
       Women—Protective law and legislation

Women—Legal status, laws, etc.—United States
  RT   Women—Civil rights—United States
  NT   Equal rights amendment (Proposed)

Women—Library resources
  NT   Feminism—Library resources

Women—Marriage-Career conflict
  USE   Women—Education—Role conflict
         Women—Employment—Role conflict

Women—Masturbation
  USE   Masturbation (Female)

Women—Monastic life
  USE   Monastic and religious life of women

Women—Monthly periods
  USE   Menstruation

Women—Occupation, Choice of
  USE   Vocational guidance for women
         Vocational guidance for women reentering employment

Women—Occupational retraining
  USE   Occupational retraining for women

Women—Occupational training
  USE   Occupational training for women

Women—Occupations
  USE   Women—Employment

Women—On the job training
  USE   Employees (Women), Training of

Women—Ordination (Christianity)
  USE   Ordination of women (Christianity)

Women—Ordination (Jewish law)
  USE   Ordination of women (Jewish law)

Women—Organizations and clubs
  USE   Women's organizations

Women—Part-time employment
  BT   Women—Employment
  RT   Part-time employment—Feminist perspective
  UF   Part-time employment—Women
         Women—Employment, Part-time

Women—Personal conduct, lifestyles, etc.

Women—Personal security
  USE   Personal security for women

Women—Physiology
  USE   Human physiology (Female)

Women—Political activism
  USE   Political activism—Women
         Politicians, Women
         Politics, Practical—Women's activism

LC **Women—Prayer books and devotions**
  Here are entered nondenominational prayer books and devotions designed
  for use primarily by women. Denominational prayer books and devotions
  are entered under the name of the religion or church; e.g. CATHOLIC CHURCH
  [CHURCH OF ENGLAND; LUTHERAN CHURCH, ETC.]—PRAYER BOOKS AND
  DEVOTIONS FOR WOMEN.
  UF   Women—Prayer books and devotions—English

Women—Prayer books and devotions—English
  USE   Women—Prayer books and devotions

Women—Prayer books and devotions—French [German, etc.]

Women—Protective law and legislation
  USE   Women—Legal status, laws, etc.—Discriminatory legislation

Women—Psychology
  BT   Psychology
  RT   Feminist psychology
         Sexism in psychology
  NT   Aggressiveness (Psychology) in women
         Assertiveness (Psychology) in women
         Body awareness training for women
         Lesbians—Psychology

LCSH: Women [Men, Children, etc.]—Conduct of life. *The LCSH heading was no doubt valid at the turn of the century, but it is somewhat out of date now.*

NT   Sex role conflict
        Sex role socialization of women
        Womanhood (Psychology)
        RAPE—PSYCHOLOGICAL ASPECTS; WOMAN BATTERING—PSYCHOLOGICAL
        ASPECTS and the subdivision PSYCHOLOGICAL ASPECTS under
        similar headings

Women—Reentry into employment
  USE   Women—Employment reentry

Women—Religious and monastic life
  USE   Monastic and religious life of women

Women—Religious life
  USE   Religion and women
        Religious life—Women

Women—Retraining, Occupational
  USE   Occupational retraining for women

Women—Security, Personal
  USE   Personal security for women

Women—Self-help health care
  USE   Women's health movement

Women—Sex role and achievement motivation
  USE   Achievement motivation and sex role of women

Women—Sex role socialization
  USE   Sex role socialization of women

Women—Sexual behavior
  USE   Sexuality—Women

LC **Women—Social conditions**
  RT   Human resources policy—Feminist perspective
  NT   Educational opportunity and women's status
        Family planning and women's status
        Girls—Social conditions
        Lesbians—Social conditions
        PROFESSIONAL WOMEN—STATUS; OFFICE WORKERS, WOMEN—STATUS
            and similar headings

Women—Societies and clubs
  USE   Women's organizations

LC **Women—Songs and music**
  NT   Feminist songs

Women—Spirituality
  USE   Feminist spirituality

Women—Sports
  USE   Sports for women

Women—Sterilization
  USE   Sterilization of women (Birth control)
        Sterilization of women (Involuntary)

Women—Subject headings
  USE   Subject headings—Women

Women—Suffrage
  BT   Women—Civil rights
  UF   Suffrage—Women

Women—Suffrage—Biography
  USE   Suffragists

Women—Training, Occupational
  USE   Occupational training for women

Women—Training on the job
  USE   Employees (Women), Training of

Women—United States
  NT   Minority women—United States
  UF   American women
        United States—Women

Women—United States—Biography
  NT   Abolitionists, Women
Women—Vocational guidance
  USE   Vocational guidance for women
        Vocational guidance for women reentering employment
Women—Voting behavior
Women—Voting rights
  USE   Women—Suffrage
Women—Wages
  USE   Wages—Women
Women—Affirmative action for
  USE   Affirmative action for women
Women, Christian
  USE   Christian women
Women, Counseling for
  USE   Counseling for women
Women, Discrimination against
  USE   Sex discrimination
Women, Divorced
  USE   Divorced women
Women, Jewish
  USE   Jewish women
Women, Jewish-American
  USE   Jewish-American women
Women, Married
  USE   Married women
Women, Middle age
  USE   Middle age women
Women, Ordination of (Christianity)
  USE   Ordination of women (Christianity)
Women, Ordination of (Jewish law)
  USE   Ordination of women (Jewish law)
Women, Personal security for
  USE   Personal security for women
Women, Poor
  USE   Poor women
Women, Professional
  USE   Professional women
Women, Senior
  USE   Senior women
Women, Single
  USE   Single women
Women, Teen age
  USE   Teen age women
Women, Unmarried
  USE   Single women
Women, Violence against
  USE   Violence against women
Women abolitionists
  USE   Abolitionists, Women
Women agricultural workers
  USE   Agricultural workers, Women
Women agriculturists
  USE   Agriculturists, Women
Women agronomists
  USE   Agriculturists, Women
Women alcoholics
  USE   Alcoholic women

Women and aggressiveness
USE   Aggressiveness (Psychology) in women

Women and assertiveness
USE   Assertiveness (Psychology) in women

Women and child custody
  BT   Child custody
  NT   Lesbians and child custody
  UF   Child custody and women

Women and Christianity
USE   Christianity and women

Women and Judaism
USE   Judaism and women

Women and Marxism
USE   Socialism and women

Women and politics
USE   Political activism—Women
        Politicians, Women
        Politics, Practical—Women's activism

Women and religion
USE   Religion and women
        Religious life—Women

Women and socialism
USE   Socialism and women

Women and the Catholic Church
USE   Catholic Church and women

Women and the Church of England
USE   Church of England and women

Women and the Vatican Counsil, 2d, 1962–1965
USE   Vatican Council, 2d, 1962–1965 and women

Women and unemployment
USE   Labor supply (Women)

Women and war
USE   War and women

Women athletics coaches
USE   Athletics coaches, Women

Women authors
USE   Authors, Women

Women bankers
USE   Bankers, Women

Women battering
USE   Woman battering

Women cantors (Jewish)
USE   Cantors, Women (Jewish)

Women church workers (Volunteer)
USE   Church workers (Volunteer), Women

Women clergy
USE   Clergywomen (Christianity)

Women clerks
USE   Clerks, Women
        Clerks (Retail trade), Women

Women coaches (Athletics)
USE   Athletics coaches, Women

Women college graduates
USE   College graduate women

Women college teachers
USE   College teachers, Women

Women counselors
USE   Counselors, Women

Women criminals
USE   Criminals, Women

Women day workers (Domestic)
USE   Household workers, Women

Women dental assistants
USE   Dental assistants, Women

Women domestics
USE   Household workers, Women

Women drunkards
USE   Alcoholic women

Women executives
USE   Executives, Women

Women farm workers
USE   Agricultural workers, Women

Women farmers
USE   Farmers, Women

Women farmworkers
USE   Agricultural workers, Women

Women filmmakers
USE   Filmmakers, Women

Women government officials
USE   Public officials, Women

Women historians
USE   Historians, Women

Women homosexuals
USE   Lesbians

Women household workers
USE   Household workers, Women

Women in Bible stories
USE   Bible stories, Women in

Women in business
USE   Businesswomen
        Executives, Women

Women in children's literature
cf.   note under WOMEN IN LITERATURE
BT   Women in literature
NT   Sex role in children's literature
        Women in Bible stories
UF   Children's literature, Women in

Women in Christianity
USE   Christianity and women

Women in church work (Volunteer)
USE   Church workers (Volunteer), Women

Women in drama
USE   Women in literature

Women in folklore and mythology
BT   Women in literature
NT   Amazons
        Witches
UF   Folklore of women
        Heroines in literature
        Mythology, Women in
        Women in mythology

Women in historiography
Here are entered works on the depiction of women and events relating to
women in historical writings. Works on women historians are entered
under HISTORIANS, WOMEN.
UF   Historiography, Women in
        History, Women in

Women in Judaism
USE   Judaism and women

LC **Women in literature**
Here are entered works which discuss the representation of women in literature. Collections of works written by women are entered under WOMEN'S WRITINGS. Works on women authors are entered under AUTHORS, WOMEN.
    NT   Feminism and feminists in literature
           Lesbians in literature
           Sex role in literature
           Women in children's literature
           Women in folklore and mythology
           Women in the Bible
    UF   Heroines in literature
           Literature, Women in
           Women in drama
           Women in poetry

Women in motion pictures
    cf.   note under WOMEN IN LITERATURE
    BT   Motion pictures
    RT   Sex role in motion pictures
    NT   Lesbians in motion pictures
    UF   Motion pictures, Women in

Women in mythology
USE   Women in folklore and mythology

Women in poetry
USE   Women in literature

Women in politics
USE   Political activism—Women
       Politicians, Women
       Politics, Practical—Women's activism

Women in religion
USE   Religion and women

Women in social work (Volunteer)
USE   Social workers (Volunteer), Women

Women in the anti-slavery movements (United States)
USE   Slavery in the United States—Anti-slavery movements—Women's
       activities

LC **Women in the Bible**
Here are entered literary works on the depiction of women in the Bible. Theological works on women's role in Biblical events are entered under WOMAN (CHRISTIAN THEOLOGY), WOMAN (JEWISH THEOLOGY)
    BT   Women in literature
    RT   Bible stories, Women in

Women in the labor force
USE   Labor supply (Women)

Women in the labor market
USE   Labor supply (Women)

Women in the professions
USE   Professional women

Women in war-time
USE   War—Civilians' work—Women
       War and women

Women labor unionists
USE   Labor unionists, Women

Women laborers
USE   Working class women—Employment

Women law paraprofessionals
USE   Law paraprofessionals, Women

LCSH practice is to assign this heading to works on the depiction of women in Bible stories for children, to literary works on the depiction of women in the Bible, and to theological works.

Women legal paraprofessionals
  USE   Law paraprofessionals, Women

Women legislators
  USE   Legislators, Women

Women librarians
  USE   Librarians, Women

Women library technicians
  USE   Library technicians, Women

Women local officials and employees
  USE   Local officials and employees, Women

Women Marxists
  USE   Socialists, Women

Women ministers
  USE   Clergywomen (Christianity)

Women offenders
  USE   Criminals, Women

Women office workers
  USE   Office workers, Women

Women paramedics
  USE   Paramedics, Women

Women paraprofessionals
  USE   Paraprofessions and paraprofessionals—Women

Women physicians
  USE   Physicians, Women

Women pioneers
  USE   Frontier and pioneer life of women
          Pioneers, Women

Women politicians
  USE   Politicians, Women

Women priests
  USE   Clergywomen (Christianity)

Women prisoners
  USE   Prisoners, Women

Women prostitutes
  USE   Prostitutes (Female)

Women public officers
  USE   Public officials, Women

Women publishers and publishing
  USE   Women's presses

Women rabbis
  USE   Rabbis, Women

Women receptionists (Office workers)
  USE   Receptionists, Women

Women sailors
  USE   Sailors, Women

Women secretaries
  USE   Secretaries, Women

Women senators (United States)
  USE   Senators (United States), Women

Women slaves (United States)
  USE   Slavery in the United States—Women slaves

Women social workers (Volunteer)
  USE   Social workers (Volunteer), Women

Women socialists
  USE   Socialists, Women

Women soldiers
  USE   Soldiers, Women

Women stenographers
  USE   Stenographers, Women

Women Strike for Peace
   BT   Vietnamese conflict, 1961–1975—Protest movements, Women's

Women trade unionists
  USE   Labor unionists, Women

Women typists
  USE   Typists, Women

Women volunteer workers
  USE   Volunteer workers, Women

Women workers
  USE   Women—Employment
          Working class women—Employment

Women workers, Volunteer
  USE   Volunteer workers, Women

Women workers' attitudes towards work
  USE   Women—Employment—Self-attitude

Women's anti-war protest movements (1961–1975)
  USE   Vietnamese conflict, 1961–1975—Protest movements, Women's

Women's apparel
  USE   Women's clothing

Women's attitudes towards work
  USE   Women—Employment—Self-attitude

Women's banks
  USE   Banks and banking, Women's

Women's bars, restaurants, etc.
   BT   Women's projects and services
   RT   Women's retreats

Women's caucuses—Trade and professional associations
  USE   Trade and professional associations—Women's caucuses

Women's centers and networks
   BT   Women's organizations
          Women's projects and services
   NT   Universities and colleges—Women's centers
          Women's health centers and clinics
   UF   Drop-in centers, Women's
          Women's drop-in centers
          Women's networks

Women's clinics
  USE   Women's health centers and clinics

Women's clothing   *LCSH:* Clothing and dress
   BT   Clothing and dress
   RT   Fashion
          Grooming for women
   UF   Apparel, Women's
          Clothing, Women's
          Women's apparel

Women's clubs
  USE   Women's organizations

Women's comic books, strips, etc.
  USE   Comic books, strips, etc., Women's

Women's comic strips
  USE   Comic books, strips, etc., Women's

Women's comix
  USE   Comic books, strips, etc., Women's

Women's consciousness-raising groups
  USE   Consciousness-raising groups, Women's

Women's crisis housing
  USE   Women's shelters

Women's cycles
  USE   Menopause
          Menstruation

Women's Day, International
USE   International Women's Day

Women's Decade, International
USE   International Women's Decade

Women's drop-in centers
USE   Women's centers and networks

Women's employment and automation
USE   Automation and women's employment

Women's film distributors
RT   Filmmakers, Women
Women's films
UF   Film distributors, Women's
Motion picture distributors, Women's

Women's films
Here are entered films made by women and films on topics of concern to women.
BT   Mass media, Women's
Motion picture
RT   Motion pictures, Nonsexist
Women's film distributors
NT   Feminist films
UF   Films, Women's
Motion pictures, Women's
Moving pictures, Women's
Women's motion pictures

Women's grooming
USE   Grooming for women

Women's health centers and clinics
BT   Women's centers and networks
Women's health movement
NT   Universities and colleges—Health services for women
UF   Clinics, Women's
Health centers, Women's
Women's clinics

Women's health movement
BT   Women's projects and services
RT   Sexism in medical care
Women—Health
NT   Women's health centers and clinics
UF   Women—Self-help health care

Women's jails
USE   Prisons for women

Women's learned periodicals
USE   Scholarly periodicals, Women's

Women's legal self-help clinics
BT   Women's projects and services
NT   Divorce—Legal self-help clinics

Women's liberation movement
USE   Women's movement (1960–   )

Women's magazines
USE   Periodicals, Women's

Women's mass media
USE   Mass media, Women's

Women's motion pictures
USE   Women's films

Women's movement (1960–   ) (Indirect)
Here are entered works on the resurgence of women's struggle for equal rights that began in the 1960's.
BT   Feminism
Social movements
UF   Women's liberation movement

The "liberation" of women was denigrated to "lib" and/or "libber" so often (as in the LCSH cross reference from Women's lib *to* Feminism) *that movement women and men have dropped the word "liberation" in referring to the movement.*

Women's movement (1960–   )—Biography
  BT   Feminists

Women's movement (1960–   )—Organizing tactics
  RT   Consciousness-raising (Technique)

Women's movement (1960–   )—Personal narratives
  BT   Feminists

Women's movement (1960–   )—United States—History
  BT   Feminism—United States—History—1960–

Women's movement (1960–   ) and economic policy
  BT   Economic policy
  UF   Women's movement (1960–   ) and public policy

Women's movement (1960–   ) and practical politics
  BT   Politics, Practical

Women's movement (1960–   ) and public policy
  USE   Women's movement (1960–   ) and economic policy
          Women's movement (1960–   ) and social policy

Women's movement (1960–   ) and social policy
  BT   Social policy
  UF   Women's movement (1960–   ) and public policy

Women's names (Personal), Change of
  USE   Married women—Personal name rights

Women's networks
  USE   Women's centers and networks

Women's newspapers
  USE   Periodicals, Women's

Women's occupations
  USE   Occupations, Women's

Women's organizations (Indirect) *LCSH:* Women—Societies and clubs
  NT   Women's centers and networks
          Women's projects and services
          Working class women's organizations
  UF   Women—Clubs
          Women—Organizations and clubs
          Women's clubs

Women's organizations—United States
  NT   African-American women's organizations
          Jewish-American women's organizations

Women's peace movements (1961–1975)
  USE   Vietnamese conflict, 1961–1975—Protest movements, Women's

Women's periodicals
  USE   Periodicals, Women's

Women's periodicals, Sexism in
  USE   Sexism in periodicals for women

Women's presses
  BT   Publishers and publishing
  RT   Feminist publishers and publishing
          Small presses
  NT   Comic books, strips, etc., Women's
  UF   Publishers and publishing, Women
          Women publishers and publishing
          Women's small presses

Women's prisons
  USE   Prisons for women

Women's projects and services
  BT   Women's organizations
  NT   Abortion clinics and referral services
          Affirmative action organizations, centers, etc.
          Anti-rape movements
          Anti-woman-battering movements
          Banks and banking, Women's

Women's projects and services (cont.)
NT Birth control clinics
Counseling for women
Feminist credit unions
Feminist psychological counseling and therapy referral services
Rape crisis centers
Teen age women's projects and services
Women's bars, restaurants, etc.
Women's centers and networks
Women's health movement
Women's legal self-help clinics
Women's shelters
UF Women's services

Women's protest movements (Anti-war) (1961–1975)
USE Vietnamese conflict, 1961–1975—Protest movements, Women's

Women's refuges
USE Women's shelters

Women's resistance and revolts
BT Women—History
NT Feminism
UF Resistance, Women's
Revolts, Women's

Women's retreats
Here are entered works on places of retirement for purposes of meditation, consciousness-raising, spiritual development, etc. Works on emergency housing for women are entered under WOMEN'S SHELTERS.
RT Women's bars, restaurants, etc.

Women's rights
USE Women—Civil rights

Women's rights feminism
USE Feminism

Women's rights to their own name
USE Married women—Personal name rights

Women's scholarly periodicals
USE Scholarly periodicals, Women's

Women's services
USE Social work with women
Women's projects and services

Women's shelters
BT Women's projects and services
RT Anti-woman-battering movement
Woman battering
UF Crisis housing, Women's
Emergency housing, Women's
Refuges, Women's
Shelters, Women's
Women's crisis housing
Women's refuges

Women's small presses
USE Women's presses

Women's status and family planning
USE Family planning and women's status

Women's studies
RT Education, Higher—Curricula, Nonsexist
Women—Education, Higher
UF Female studies
Feminist studies
Studies of women
Women studies

Women's studies—Periodicals
BT Periodicals, Women's

Women's studies—Study and teaching

Women's suffrage
  USE   Women—Suffrage

Women's work in war-time
  USE   War—Civilians' work—Women

LC **Women's writings**
    cf.   note under WOMEN IN LITERATURE

Women's Year, International
  USE   International Women's Year

Workers
  USE   Working classes—Employment

Workers—Wages
  USE   Wages

Workers, Agricultural
  USE   Agricultural workers

Workers, Domestic
  USE   Household workers

Workers, Farm
  USE   Agricultural workers

Workers' attitudes toward women coworkers
  USE   Women—Employment—Attitudes of men

Working class men
  BT   Men
        Working classes

Working class women
  BT   Women
        Working classes
  NT   Working class women's organizations

Working class women—Employment
  RT   Labor unionists, Women
  NT   Agricultural workers, Women
        Household workers, Women
  UF   Women laborers
        Women workers

Working class women's organizations
  BT   Women's organizations
        Working class women

Working classes
Here are entered general and theoretical works on the working class.
Works on working class employment are entered under WORKING CLASSES—EMPLOYMENT.
  NT   Working class men
        Working class women
  UF   Laboring classes

Working classes—Employment
  RT   Labor unions
  NT   Agricultural workers
        Household workers
        White collar workers
  UF   Laborers
        Workers

Working mothers
  USE   Mothers—Employment

Working wives
  USE   Married women—Employment

World economics
  USE   Economic policy

World leaders
  NT   Politicians

LCSH: Labor and laboring classes, *but cf. LCSH* Middle classes *and* Upper classes. *LC does not use the subdivision* Employment *under* Labor and laboring classes; *as a consequence works on labor, general works on working class people, and works on working class employment are not distinguished from one another.*

LC **World War, 1939–1945**
    UF   European War, 1939–1945

World war, 1939–1945—Civilians' work
    BT   War—Civilians' work
    NT   World War, 1939–1945—Civilians' work, Industrial
           World War, 1939–1945—Civilians' work, Volunteer
    UF   World War, 1939–1945—Defense work, Civilian

World War, 1939–1945—Civilians' work—Women
    NT   World War, 1939–1945—Civilians' work, Industrial—Women
           World War, 1939–1945—Civilians' work, Volunteer—Women
    UF   World War, 1939–1945—Women's work

World War, 1939–1945—Civilians' work, Industrial
    UF   World War, 1939–1945—Industrial civilian defense work

World War, 1939–1945—Civilians' work, Industrial—Women
    BT   World War, 1939–1945—Civilians' work—Women

World War, 1939–1945—Civilians' work, Volunteer
    UF   World War, 1939–1945—Volunteer civilian defense work

World War, 1939–1945—Civilians' work, Volunteer—Women
    BT   World War, 1939–1945—Civilians' work—Women

World War, 1939–1945—Defense work, Civilian
  USE   World War, 1939–1945—Civilians' work

World War, 1939–1945—Industrial civilian defense work
  USE   World War, 1939–1945—Civilians' work, Industrial

World War, 1939–1945—Volunteer civilian defense work
  USE   World War, 1939–1945—Civilians' work, Volunteer

World War, 1939–1945—Women's work
  USE   World war, 1939–1945—Civilians' work—Women

Youth
  USE   Teen age

During the examination of LC's catalog it became obvious that the numerous works on women's contribution to the WWII war effort were entered only under Women—Employment. *The subdivision* Women's work *under WWII was used for volunteer women's work, not for the ''Rosie the riviter'' kind of work. After some searching (there are no references from civilian defense work) works on civilians' ''paid'' contributions to the war effort were found entered under the subdivision* Manpower. *Perhaps it is because the subdivision specifies* man*power that works on* woman*power were entered only under* Women—Employment. *Obviously, Rosie was not really doing* her *work; she should have been home knitting sweaters or out serving doughnuts.*